別冊　問題

大学入試　全レベル問題集

英語長文

3 ｜ 私大標準レベル

三訂版

JN047132

Obunsha

大学入試　全レベル問題集　英語長文
レベル３［三訂版］　別冊（問題編）

目　次

編集部より

問題を解くときには英文音声は必要ありませんが，復習の際にはぜひ音声を利用して英
文の通し聞きを繰り返しおこなってください。語彙やイントネーションの定着に，音声
を介したインプットは非常に効果的です。

次の英文を読んで，あとの問いに答えなさい。

　　A vast stretch of land lies untouched by civilization in the back country of the eastern portion of the African continent. (　ア　) the occasional exception of a big-animal hunter, foreigners never enter this area.　Aside from the Wandorobo* tribe, even the natives stay away from this particular area because it is the home of the deadly tsetse fly*.　The tribe depend on the forest for their lives, eating its roots and fruits and making their homes (　イ　) they find themselves at the end of the day.　One of the things they usually eat is honey. They obtain it through an ancient, symbiotic* relationship with a bird known as the Indicator.　The scientific community finally confirmed the report that this bird intentionally led the natives to trees containing the honey of wild bees.　Other species of honey guides are also known to take advantage of the search efforts of some animals in much the same way (　ウ　) the Indicator uses men.

　　This amazing bird settles in a tree near a Wandorobo camp and sings incessantly* until the men answer it with whistles.　It then begins its leading flight.　Singing, it hops from tree to tree, (　エ　) the men continue their musical answering call.　When the bird reaches the tree, its voice becomes shriller* and its followers examine the tree carefully. The Indicator usually sits just over the bees' nests, and the men hear the sounds of the bees in the hollow trunk*. (　オ　) fire, they smoke most of the bees out of the tree, but those that escape the effects of the smoke attack the men violently.　In spite of the attack, the Wandorobos gather the honey and leave a small gift for their bird guide.

*Wandorobo：ワンドロボ族（ケニアやタンザニアの高地に住む狩猟採集部族）

　tsetse fly：ツェツェバエ（アフリカ産のイエバエの一種）

　symbiotic：共生の

　incessantly：絶え間なく，間断なく

　shrill(er)：（より）鋭い

　hollow trunk：内部が空になっている木の幹

問 本文中の空所（ア）～（オ）に入る最も適切なものをそれぞれ①～④の中から１つ選びなさい。

（ア）　① At　　　　② With　　　③ For　　　④ Of

（イ）　① wherever　② however　③ whenever　④ whoever

（ウ）　① as　　　　② which　　　③ but　　　④ who

（エ）　① for　　　　② that　　　③ unless　　④ while

（オ）　① Use　　　② To use　　③ Using　　④ Used

次の英文を読んで，あとの問いに答えなさい。

Each year on December 10, the world's attention turns to Sweden for the announcement of the Nobel Prize winners. The Nobel Prizes, six prizes given to groups or individuals who really stand out in their fields, were founded by a Swedish inventor, Alfred Nobel.

(ア)Alfred Nobel was the man who invented dynamite, a powerful explosive. During his life, Nobel made a lot of money from his invention, and he decided that he wanted to use his money to help scientists, artists, and people who worked to help others around the world. When he died, his will said that the money would be placed in a bank, and the interest the money earned would be given out as five annual cash prizes.

The prizes set up by Nobel were first handed out in 1901, and included physics, medicine, chemistry, literature, and peace. (イ)Later, in 1968 the Bank of Sweden* added a prize in economics to celebrate the bank's 300th year of business.

Each person who receives a Nobel Prize is given a cash prize, a medal, and a certificate. The prize money for each category is currently worth about a million dollars, and the aim of the prize is to allow the winner to carry on working or researching without having to worry about raising money.

The prizes can be given to either individuals or (ウ)groups. Prize winners include Albert Einstein (physics, 1921), Kenzaburo Oe (literature, 1994), Kim Dae Jung (peace, 2001), the United Nations (peace, 2001), and Nelson Mandela (peace, 1993).

The prize winner that has won the most times is the International Committee for the Red Cross. (エ)This organization has received three Nobel Peace Prizes (in 1917, 1944, and 1963), and the founder, Jean Henri Dunant, was awarded the first Nobel Peace Prize, in 1901.

＊the Bank of Sweden：スウェーデン国立銀行

問1 次の英文①〜⑧の中から，本文の内容に一致するものを5つ選びなさい。

① The Nobel Prizes are given to people around the world who worked with Alfred Nobel.

② Alfred Nobel was an inventor and set up the Nobel Prizes.

③ In 1901, six Nobel Prizes were first handed out.

④ A prize in economics was later added.

⑤ Nobel Prize winners are given three things that include money.

⑥ Kim Dae Jung, Kenzaburo Oe, and Nelson Mandela are all peace prize winners.

⑦ The International Committee of the Red Cross was founded by Jean Henri Dunant.

⑧ Jean Henri Dunant was one of the first Nobel Prize winners in 1901.

問2 下線部(ウ)(エ)について，それぞれの下線部が含まれる段落から英語で抜き出して答えなさい。

(ウ) groups とありますが，ノーベル賞を受賞した団体を1つ英語で書きなさい。

_____

(エ) This organization とありますが，その名前を英語で書きなさい。

_____

6

問3 賞金の目的が文中に書かれていますが，それは何ですか。簡潔に日本語で説明しなさい。

_____

_____

問4 下線部（ア）（イ）を日本語に直しなさい。

（ア）_____

_____

（イ）_____

_____

次の英文を読んで，あとの問いに答えなさい。

Why would someone decide to stop eating? We know that the body needs food in order to function well. However, many people (ア)fast at some time during their lives. Why is this?

Some people fast for political reasons. In the early 20th century, women in England and the United States weren't allowed to vote. In （ イ ）, many women went on fasts. They hoped that fasting would bring attention to (ウ)this injustice. Mohandas Gandhi, the famous Indian leader, fasted 17 times during his life. For Gandhi, fasting was a powerful political tool. In 1943, he fasted to bring attention to his country's need for independence. For 21 days, he went without food. Another famous faster was Cesar Chavez. In the 1960s, he fasted for three weeks. Why? His goal was to bring attention to the terrible working conditions of farm workers in the United States.

Fasting is also a spiritual practice in many religions. Every year during the month of Ramadan, which is a religious holiday, Muslims fast from sunrise to sunset. Many Hindus fast on special occasions, (エ)as do some Christians and Buddhists.

Of course, not everyone fasts for political or religious reasons. Some people occasionally fast just because it makes them feel better. The American writer Mark Twain thought fasting was the best （ オ ） for common illnesses. Whenever he had a cold or a fever, he stopped eating completely. He said that this always made his cold or fever go away. Another American writer, Upton Sinclair, discovered fasting after years of overeating, stomach problems, and headaches. His first fast lasted for 12 days. During this time, his headaches and stomachaches went away. Sinclair said that fasting also made him more alert and energetic.

Choosing to go without food can be very dangerous. However, that doesn't stop people from fasting for political, religious, or health reasons.

問 1 下線部(ア)の意味として最も適切なものを①〜④の中から 1 つ選べ。

① hurry home

② eat nothing

③ run away from home

④ live and work for nothing

問 2 空所(イ)を満たすものとして最も適切なものを①〜④の中から 1 つ選べ。

① turn　　　② detail　　　③ protest　　　④ competition

問 3 下線部(ウ)が指示する内容として最も適切なものを①〜④の中から 1 つ選べ。

① 選挙権がなかったこと

② 食べ物が十分得られなかったこと

③ 労働環境が悪かったこと

④ 教会で結婚することが許されなかったこと

問 4 下線部(エ)の指示する内容として最も適切なものを①〜④の中から 1 つ選べ。

① some Christians and Buddhists also go to church or temple

② some Christians and Buddhists also fast on special occasions

③ some Christians and Buddhists also work from sunrise to sunset

④ some Christians and Buddhists also take part in volunteer activities

問5 空所(オ)を満たすのに最も適切なものを①~④の中から 1 つ選べ。

① food   ② seller   ③ place   ④ medicine

問6 本文の表題として最も適切なものを①~④の中から 1 つ選べ。

① Diet and Health

② Eating Moderately

③ Living in Good Health

④ Reasons for Going without Food

問7 本文の内容と一致するものを①~⑦の中から 3 つ選べ。

① We must be physically active to keep extra calories out of the body.

② Mohandas Gandhi did not fast as a political tool.

③ Cesar Chavez fasted for political reasons.

④ Mark Twain believed fasting was a useful way of getting rid of a cold.

⑤ Upton Sinclair used to eat a lot and suffer from stomach troubles.

⑥ People today no longer fast.

⑦ Fasting is dangerous except for patients suffering from medical problems.

次の英文を読んで，あとの問いに答えなさい。

Many people don't know that the difference between success and failure is often very small. One does not need to be twice as good, let alone perfect, in order to succeed in most things. In fact, often only a tiny difference separates winners and losers. A small difference may make a big difference. This is true in many areas of life, especially if the small difference is regular and repeated.

For example, consider two clocks, running at a speed differing only by one second per hour. Only one second per hour doesn't seem like much, but it is almost a half minute per day, or almost three minutes a week, or about twelve minutes a month, and almost two and a half hours a year. Well, there's actually quite a difference between those two clocks.

Sports is another good example. One doesn't have to be much better than others to win. The difference between winning and losing is often very small. At the Olympics, the difference between winning and losing is often just 0.1 second or just a centimeter or two. Such a small difference can determine who gets a gold medal.

A small difference, often just a percent or two, if repeated over and over, will almost always lead to success in the future. One does not need to be a genius, does not need to be ten times better, or even twice as good, let alone perfect. Just a small difference is usually enough to succeed.

Our heroes seem to have superpowers, but actually they are just normal people. They are not really that much different from us. They are just a tiny bit faster, or smarter, or more beautiful than average. If one wants to be successful, just remember that the difference between success and failure is often very small. So why don't you try just a little harder, a little more often? A small difference may make a big difference. You may be surprised by the result.

問1 What don't many people know?

① A small success is often different from failure.

② Failure and success are often different.

③ There is often a small difference between success and failure.

④ Failure is often a small success.

問2 A person who wins a gold medal is often someone who _____.

① is ten times faster

② is twice as fast

③ is just a little faster

④ never gives up

問3 "A small difference may make a big difference" means _____.

① success often depends on a little luck

② success often depends on small things

③ never give up

④ life is often true

問4 The difference between winners and losers is often _____ .

① quite a bit

② a lot

③ twice as good

④ not much

問5 According to the story, _____ usually leads to success.

① being mostly better just a little of the time

② being a lot better most of the time

③ repeating just a percent or two

④ being perfect in the future

問6 According to the story, we can be more successful if _____ .

① we are a genius

② we are ten times better

③ we are perfect

④ we are just a little better

問7 Heroes _____.

① have superpowers

② are successful because they are usually a bit better

③ are much different from others

④ are not really more beautiful than average

問8 At the end of the first paragraph, the expression "the small difference is regular and repeated" means _____.

① practice over and over

② a small difference is often just a percent or two

③ a small difference

④ a series of small differences

問9 The word "result" at the end of the story refers to _____.

① your success

② your effort

③ trying harder

④ a small failure

問10 What's the best title for this story?

① Practice Makes Perfect

② A Small Success

③ How to Succeed

④ How Not to Make a Difference

次の英文を読んで，あとの問いに答えなさい。

　　In the early 1940s, on the night of her graduation party, a high school girl named Doris Van Kappelhoff was involved in a serious car accident. She had planned to go to Hollywood to become a dancer in films, but her injuries made that future no longer possible. During her long recovery at home, Doris began to sing along with the female vocalists on the radio. Her voice became so well trained that she was hired to sing in a band, and soon thereafter, she found parts in movies, changing her name to Doris Day. Her original plans were destroyed by a tragic event, but thereby she found her true calling. Things don't always go according to our plans, but a change of plans may be an example of coincidental circumstances that lead us to a fulfilling life, unguessed and unsought — a blessing from God.

　　We make plans expecting to be in control of what will happen. Perhaps we fear natural happenings, things turning out contrary to our wishes. The course of life is challenging if we are concerned with trying to control it. We may act with precision, and self-discipline, expecting the world to do the same and give us what we want, but that is rarely the case.

　　Perfect discipline, or perfect control, is the most certain way to miss out on the joy of life. The unexpectedness of life means that we are free not to plan perfectly. We can flow into the natural chaos of life, so untidy, so unpredictable, or we can try to order life fully by making careful plans. But as Rover Burns says, "The best-prepared schemes often go wrong and leave us nothing but grief and pain for promised joy."

　　Making plans is an adult occupation, a feature of a

healthy ego. However, life often does not proceed according to our plans. This does not have to leave us disappointed. Perhaps we believe the universe has a plan that more accurately reflects our emerging destiny.

問 空所に入れるのに最も適切なものを選びなさい。

(ア) Doris Van Kappelhoff _____ .

① was injured in a car accident on her way to the graduation ceremony

② wanted to direct Hollywood movies in the future

③ gave up becoming a dancer in Hollywood movies

④ was hospitalized for several years

(イ) Doris improved her singing skills by _____ .

① singing along with the female singers on the radio

② acting her parts in Hollywood movies

③ being hired to sing in a professional band

④ finding her true calling

(ウ) The author believes we _____ .

① are trying to control how other people behave

② can never know completely what will happen in our lives

③ rarely fear things will happen contrary to our wishes

④ should expect the world will give us our reward

(エ) What Rover Burns means is that _____.

    ① we can improve our lives if we make the best plans

    ② we often have to lead a miserable life if we are unlucky

    ③ even the best plan may lead to a sad and painful end

    ④ the best plan will prevent us from falling into disappointment

(オ) The best title for this passage is _____.

    ① "Life Is Not Always Fair"

    ② "How to Receive the Feeling of Others"

    ③ "People Are Not Loving and Loyal All the Time"

    ④ "Things Do Not Always Go According to the Plan"

次の英文を読んで，あとの問いに答えなさい。

　　Hunting for a job is a painful experience, but one that nearly everyone must endure at least once in a lifetime. Books are published and magazine articles are written on the subject, all trying to tell job-seekers what they should do or avoid doing （　ア　） to survive and to win the game. They can't calm the nervous applicant (and what applicant is not nervous?), but they do offer some advice that deserves consideration.

　　To begin with, it is not a good idea to be late. Job interviewers don't think very highly of the candidate who arrives twenty minutes after the appointed time, offering no apology or explaining that he couldn't find the street, and that his watch is slow. The wise job-seeker explores the place the day before to make sure that he can locate the building, the right floor, and the office in which the interview is to take place; at the same time he looks around to see what the employees are wearing and how they seem to behave at work. Next day he arrives early for the appointment. It does not matter if the employer's secretary recognizes him and mentions his first visit to her boss. （　イ　） the eager candidate can only be regarded as smart, thoughtful, and well-organized — three points in his favor before he has said a word.

　　Most personnel managers admit that they know within the first few minutes of the meeting whether or not they want to hire the person to whom they are talking. This is particularly true when their first reaction to the applicant is negative, when the man or woman has made a disastrous first impression. But what makes a *good* impression? What counts? Being on time does, as we have seen; then, appearance. It is (ウ) for the candidate to be dressed properly, and to look alert, pleasant, and interested. It is also very important to look the interviewer in the eyes because this "eye contact" gives a strong impression of sincerity and openness.

問1 本文中の空所 (ア)〜(ウ) に入る最も適切なものを①〜④から1つずつ選びなさい。

(ア) ① in order ② with regard

③ in the end ④ with reference

(イ) ① However, ② What is more,

③ On the contrary, ④ Accordingly,

(ウ) ① formal ② essential

③ genuine ④ valid

(ア) [   ] (イ) [   ] (ウ) [   ]

問2 次の (エ)〜(カ) が本文の内容と一致するように，最も適切なものを①〜④から1つずつ選び，英文を完成しなさい。

(エ) Books on hunting for a job _____

① are painful to read.

② list likely employers.

③ make people nervous.

④ give useful guidance.

[   ]

(オ) Job applicants should _____

① avoid being recognized if they arrive in advance.

② visit the office a day early to avoid getting lost.

③ arrive after the appointed time to be regarded as smart.

④ mention their thoughts about employees' clothing and behavior.

[   ]

（カ） It's important to make a good first impression because _____

① managers make their hiring decisions very quickly.

② candidates are dressed well and are interested.

③ interviewers are impressed by sincere "eye-contact".

④ applicants otherwise react negatively.

次の英文を読んで，あとの問いに答えなさい。

　　We've used the wind as an energy source for a long time. The Babylonians and Chinese were using wind power to pump water for irrigating crops 4,000 years ago, and sailing boats were around long before that. Wind power was used in the Middle Ages, in Europe, to （　ア　） corn, which is where the term "windmill" comes from.

　　The sun heats our atmosphere unevenly, so some parts become warmer than others. These warm parts rise up, other air blows in to replace them — and we feel a wind blowing. We can use the energy in the wind by building a tall tower, （　イ　） a large propeller on the top. The wind blows the propeller round, which turns a generator to produce electricity. We tend to （　ウ　） many of these towers together, to make a "wind farm" and produce more electricity. The more towers, the more wind, and the larger the propellers, the more electricity we can make. It's only worth building wind farms in places that have strong, steady winds.

　　The best places for wind farms are in coastal areas, （　エ　） the tops of rounded hills, on open plains and in gaps in mountains — places where the wind is strong and reliable. Some are offshore. To be worthwhile, you need an average wind speed of around 25 km/h. Most wind farms in the UK are in Cornwall or Wales. Isolated places （　オ　） farms may have their own wind generators. Several wind farms supply electricity to homes around Los Angeles in California.

　　The propellers are large, to take energy out from the largest possible volume of air. The angle of the blades can be changed, to cope with varying wind speeds, and the generator and propeller can turn to face the wind wherever it comes from. Some designs use vertical turbines, which don't need to be turned to face the wind. The towers are tall, to get the propellers as high as possible, up to where the wind is stronger. This means that the land beneath can still be used for farming.

(ア) ① steam   ② grind   ③ peel

(イ) ① of   ② with   ③ towards

(ウ) ① build   ② blow   ③ convert

(エ) ① at   ② in   ③ under

(オ) ① likely to   ② which are   ③ such as

問2 次の①〜⑤の英文を読んで，本文に照らして正しいものに〇，間違って
いるものに×をつけなさい。

① European people were the first to use wind power in agriculture.

② The cause of wind lies in the difference of temperature in some parts
of the air.

③ A wind farm is constructed in places where wind is stronger.

④ Most wind farms are situated offshore.

⑤ Vertical turbines turn the generator and propeller to face the wind.

次の英文を読んで，あとの問いに答えなさい。

Phillis Wheatley was (**ア** bear) in Senegal. She arrived in America on a slave ship around 1761, when she was seven or eight years old, and was purchased in Boston by John Wheatley, who wanted a personal （ **イ**) for his wife, Susanna Wheatley. When the Wheatleys' daughter saw Phillis trying to write the alphabet with chalk on the wall, she (**ウ** teach) her to read. (エ)<u>Within a year and a half, Phillis was fluent in English and had also begun to study Latin.</u> By the time she was thirteen she was writing poetry. Her work began to appear in New England newspapers, and she became a regional celebrity. She had found a way out of the normal restrictions of her (**オ** assign) role in life through poetry.

(**カ** treat) more as a daughter than a servant by the Wheatley family, Phillis became known for her dignity and conversation as well as her writings. In Britain, the Countess of Huntington admired one of her poems, and arranged the publication of a book by (キ)<u>a very extraordinary female slave.</u> The high point of Phillis Wheatley's life came in 1773, when she traveled to England, where she was taken up by the literary celebrities of the day and invited to be presented at court. But the illness of Susanna Wheatley cut short her visit, and Phillis returned to （ **ク**), where her mistress died and John Wheatley officially freed her.

She was the first American writer to achieve international （ **ケ**). Benjamin Franklin read her work, which sometimes compared the experience of a slave to that of American colonists under British tyranny. George Washington invited her to visit him at his camp during the War of

Independence. Some historians credit her with Washington's decision to allow black men to serve in his army.

Phillis Wheatley found no happiness in her own (コ). She continued to live with her old master until his death, but the people of Boston had much less interest in her as a free black woman than they did when she was the beloved (サ) of a prominent white family.

問1 下線部(エ)を和訳しなさい。

_____

_____

問2 下線部(キ)は誰を指しているのか, その人物の名前を本文中から探して書きなさい。

_____

問3 (ア)(ウ)(オ)(カ)の中の語を適切な形に変えなさい。解答はすべて1語で答えなさい。

(ア) [　　　　] **(ウ)** [　　　　]

(オ) [　　　　] **(カ)** [　　　　]

問4 空所(イ)(ク)(ケ)(コ)(サ)の中に入るべき文脈上最も適切な語を1語選びなさい。

(イ) ① friend ② servant ③ writer [　　　]

(ク) ① Boston ② London ③ Senegal [　　　]

(ケ) ① famc ② freedom ③ journey [　　　]

(コ) ① activity ② liberty ③ slavery [　　　]

(サ) ① liberated ② slave ③ writer [　　　]

問5 次の①～⑦の中で本文の内容と一致する事柄を述べている文には○, 一致しない文には×を書きなさい。

① Phillis came to America in the mid-seventeenth century.

② Mr. and Mrs. Wheatley had no children and took Phillis as their own daughter.

③ Phillis was not good at English when she came to America.

④ Phillis worked for New England newspapers.

⑤ The Wheatleys didn't like Phillis very much even though she was a good servant.

⑥ Mrs. Wheatley freed Phillis on her death bed.

⑦ Some black men fought for the independence of America.

次の英文を読んで，あとの問いに答えなさい。

Growing up without language

It is almost impossible for us to imagine growing up without language, which develops in our minds (ア)<u>so effortlessly</u> in early childhood and plays such a central role in defining us as human and allowing us to (イ)<u>participate in</u> our culture. Nevertheless, being (ウ)<u>deprived of</u> language occasionally happens. In recent centuries children have been found living in the wild, said to have been raised by wolves or other animals and deprived of human contact. It is hard to know the real stories behind these cases, but they are all (エ)<u>strikingly</u> similar with respect to language. The pattern is that only those rescued early in childhood developed an ability to speak. Those found after they were about nine years old learned only a few words, or failed to learn language at all.

One of the most famous of these cases is that of Victor, "the wild boy of Aveyron," made famous in a film by François Truffaut called *The Wild Child*. Victor was captured in 1800, when he was about ten or eleven. He was studied by a young physician named Jean Itard, who creatively and (オ)<u>painstakingly</u> tried to teach him to speak, read, and write. But despite Itard's best efforts, Victor never learned to speak; he learned to read and print only a small set of words.

Children without hearing are not as handicapped. A deaf child can still have language and relate normally to others through signing — (カ)<u>as long as</u> language development starts early. There are a number of studies that show that the sooner a deaf child (キ)<u>is exposed to</u> a natural sign language, such as American Sign Language, the more (ク)<u>proficient</u> a signer he or she will become. As in other cases of linguistic isolation, the ability of deaf people to learn new *words* is not (ケ)affected by the age at which they are exposed to language. But their ability to learn grammar is dramatically affected. Studies of deaf children exposed to sign language after the preschool years show that there is (コ)a critical period for grammatical development, which ends, perhaps, in the early school-age years.

問1 上記英文中の下線部(ア)〜(コ)の意味内容として最も適切なものを，それぞれ①〜④から1つ選びなさい。

(ア) so effortlessly
① so often   ② with so much trouble
③ so easily   ④ with so little reason

(イ) participate in
① play a role in   ② create
③ do well at   ④ teach

(ウ) deprived of
① added to   ② denied contact with
③ led up to   ④ stolen from

(エ) strikingly
① usually   ② very   ③ partly   ④ in no way

（オ） <u>painstakingly</u>

① for a long time   ② innocently

③ in various ways   ④ taking a lot of trouble

（カ） <u>as long as</u>

① while   ② as well as

③ provided that   ④ in the same way

（キ） <u>is exposed to</u>

① shows   ② is bought   ③ masters   ④ has contact with

（ク） <u>proficient</u>

① skillful   ② realistic   ③ entertaining   ④ fortunate

（ケ） <u>affected</u>

① improved   ② influenced   ③ shown   ④ understood

（コ） <u>a critical</u>

① a large   ② an open   ③ an important   ④ a shallow

問2 下記の文章①〜⑨の中で本文の内容に一致するものを3つ選びなさい（順序は問わない）。

① No child ever misses out on learning a language in order to communicate.

② Language is one of the main things that make us human.

③ Children can start learning a language successfully at any age.

④ After much hard work, Victor learned to speak a few words.

⑤ Itard succeeded in teaching Victor to read a little but not to speak.

⑥ Deaf children are worse off than children isolated from language.

⑦ It's easier for deaf children or children isolated from language to learn grammar than vocabulary.

⑧ Sign language is of no use to deaf children.

⑨ It's essential to learn grammar by a relatively early age.

次の英文を読んで，あとの問いに答えなさい。

A star is a big ball of fire in space that makes lots of light and other forms of energy. A star is mostly made up of gases and something like fire, only much hotter. There are thousands of explosions happening all over the star all the time. This is where the star's heat and light come from. These explosions are also where a star gets its color from.

Our sun is a star. It is the closest star to our planet, and it sends its energy to the Earth as heat and light. The sun seems large to us, but it is only a medium-sized star called a yellow dwarf (small star). Other stars can be different colors. Some stars have more energy than our sun and burn even hotter than our sun does. Stars that are hotter than our sun may look blue or white. Stars that are cooler than our sun may look orange or red.

Stars come in many sizes. Our sun is about 1.4 million kilometers around, but people still call it a dwarf because many stars are much bigger. For example, there are many stars which are more than 100 times bigger than our sun. The largest stars are called red supergiants. These stars are so big that most of our small solar system would fit inside one. (ア)If our sun turned into a red supergiant, the outside of the sun would be past Jupiter's orbit.

Stars, just like people, have a life, but a star's life is much longer than a human's life. The sun is millions of years old and will live for many more millions of years. When our sun starts to die, it will grow into a red giant star. (イ)It will not become a supergiant because it is not heavy enough. When our sun dies, it will get so hot that the heat and light will burn the Earth. In fact, it will be too hot for anything to live on the Earth when our sun becomes a red giant. Then, our sun will slowly get darker and colder until it stops giving off any energy at all.

問1 本文の第1段落の内容に合うものとして最も適当なものを，①〜④から1つ選べ。

① Some stars do not have any explosions because they have no gases.

② Stars usually have less than one thousand explosions on their surface.

③ The star's color is not related to the explosions around the star.

④ The star's heat and light are caused by explosions on it.

問2 本文の第2段落の内容に合うものとして最も適当なものを，①〜④から1つ選べ。

① Compared with the sun, stars that look orange are much hotter.

② Stars may look blue when they have a lower temperature than the sun.

③ There are no stars which burn much hotter than the sun.

④ There are some stars which produce more energy than the sun.

問3 下線部(ア)の内容として最も適当なものを，①〜④から１つ選べ。

① If the sun became a red supergiant, Jupiter would be far from the sun.

② If the sun changed into a red supergiant, Jupiter's orbit would be inside the sun.

③ If the sun hit a red supergiant, Jupiter would not exist anymore.

④ If the sun went around a red supergiant, it would be close to Jupiter.

問4 本文の第３段落の内容に合うものとして最も適当なものを，①〜④から１つ選べ。

① Dwarf stars cannot be as large as the sun.

② One of the biggest stars in space is the sun.

③ Red supergiants are a type of dwarf star.

④ There are a lot of different-sized stars.

問5 下線部(イ)の内容として最も適当なものを，①〜④から１つ選べ。

① As it gains weight, the sun will slowly grow into a supergiant.

② Because of its weight, the sun cannot be a supergiant.

③ The sun can get as big as a supergiant because it is heavy.

④ The sun will become a supergiant when it loses enough weight.

問6 本文の第4段落の内容に合うものとして最も適当なものを，①～④から1つ選べ。

① After it becomes a red giant, the sun will quickly get cold and dark.

② Creatures on the Earth will survive after the sun becomes a red giant.

③ The sun continues to produce heat and light forever even after it dies.

④ When the sun dies, the temperature of the Earth will get much higher.

問7 本文の内容に合わないものを，①～⑦から2つ選べ。

① The forms of energy that the Earth gets from the sun are heat and light.

② The Earth is heated mainly by the energy produced by a red supergiant.

③ The sun is much bigger than all the other stars called "yellow dwarfs."

④ The temperatures of white stars and red stars are not the same.

⑤ Many stars in space are more than one hundred times the size of the sun.

⑥ The sun is expected to continue to exist for millions of years more.

⑦ The sun can become a giant star but not a supergiant.

次の英文を読んで、あとの問いに答えなさい。

If you have experienced unwanted weight gain or weight loss during the pandemic, you are not alone. According to a poll by the American Psychological Association, 61% of U.S. adults reported (ア)undesired weight change since the pandemic began.

The results, released in March 2021, showed that during the pandemic, 42% of respondents gained unwanted weight — 29 pounds on average — and nearly 10% of those people gained more than 50 pounds. (イ), nearly 18% of Americans said they experienced unwanted weight loss — on average, a loss of 26 pounds.

Another study, published on March 22, 2021, assessed weight change in 269 people from February to June 2020. The researchers found, on average, that people gained a steady 1.5 pounds per month.

I am a nutritional neuroscientist, and my research investigates the relationship between (ウ)diet, lifestyle, stress and mental distress such as anxiety and depression.

The common denominator to changes in body weight, especially during a pandemic, is stress. The findings about unwanted weight changes make sense in a stressful world, especially in the context of the body's stress response, better known as the fight-or-flight response.

The fight-or-flight response is an (エ)innate reaction that evolved as a survival mechanism. It empowers humans to react swiftly to acute stress — like a predator — or adapt to chronic stress — like a food shortage. When faced with stress, the body wants to keep the brain alert. It decreases levels of some hormones and brain chemicals in order to turn down behaviors that won't help in an urgent situation, and it increases other hormones that will.

When under stress, the body lowers levels of neurotransmitters such as serotonin, dopamine and melatonin. Serotonin regulates emotions, appetite and digestion. So, low levels of serotonin increase anxiety and can change a person's eating habits. Dopamine — another feel-good neurotransmitter — regulates goal-oriented motivation. Dwindling levels of dopamine can translate into lower motivation to exercise, maintain a healthy lifestyle or perform daily tasks.

Overall, stress can throw your eating habits and motivation to exercise or eat healthy way out of balance, and this last year has certainly been a stressful one for everyone.

So why did people gain or lose weight this last year? And what explains the dramatic differences?

Many people find comfort in (オ) food. That is because chocolate and other sweets can make you happy by boosting serotonin levels in the short term. However, the blood clears the extra sugar very quickly, so the mental boost is extremely short-lived, leading people to eat more. Eating for comfort can be a natural response to stress, but when combined with the lower motivation to exercise and consumption of low-nutrient, calorie-dense food, stress can result in unwanted weight gain.

What about weight loss? (カ)<u>In a nutshell</u>, the brain is connected to the gut through a two-way communication system called the vagus nerve. When you are stressed, your body inhibits the signals that travel through the vagus nerve and slows down the digestive process. When this happens, people experience fullness.

The pandemic left many people confined to their homes, bored and with plenty of food and little to distract them. When adding the stress factor to this scenario, you have a perfect situation for unwanted weight changes. Stress will always be a part of life, but there are things you can do — like practicing positive self-talk — that can help ward off the stress response and some of its unwanted consequences.

*Lina Begdache, "Unwanted Weight Gain or Weight Loss during the Pandemic? Blame Your Stress Hormones," *The Conversation.* 2 April 2021, https://theconversation.com/unwanted-weight-gain-or-weight-loss-during-the-pandemic-blame-your-stress-hormones-157852 より

問1 この話の流れで下線部(ア)undesired という言葉が使われる理由として最も適切なものを①〜④の中から 1 つ選びなさい。

① To make the participants of the poll feel better about the change in their weight.

② Because some of these adults were planning to lose weight before the pandemic.

③ Because the adults who experienced a change in weight were completely satisfied with their body shape.

④ To highlight the difference between an accidental change in weight and an intentional change in weight.

問2 文脈から考えて，空所(**イ**)に入る表現として最も適切な語句を①〜④の中から1つ選びなさい。

① On the one hand　　② In the end

③ In addition to　　④ On the flip side

問3 第1段落〜第3段落(If you have ... pounds per month.)の内容と一致する文を①〜④の中から1つ選びなさい。

① Many Americans experienced weight gain due to excessive eating.

② Studies revealed that many Americans experienced weight change during the pandemic.

③ Both studies tracked weight change from February to June 2020.

④ According to the studies, more people experienced weight loss rather than weight gain during the pandemic.

問4 下線部(**ウ**)diet と同じ意味で使われているものを①〜④の中から1つ選びなさい。

① My friend Allison is dieting because she will have a health check at the end of the month.

② Lawmakers have been debating changes to the immigration law in the Diet for weeks.

③ Some habits you should keep to stay fit are regular exercise and a healthy diet.

④ This TV channel only offers a diet of bad reality shows and cooking programs.

問5 下線部(エ)innate の言い換えとして最も適切なものを①～④の中から1つ選びなさい。

① expected   ② natural   ③ quick   ④ transparent

問6 第5段落～第7段落(The common denominator ... perform daily tasks.)の内容と一致する文を①～④の中から1つ選びなさい。

① When human beings face stressful situations, they start paying more attention to their appearance.

② Excessive stress causes the brain to produce more neurotransmitters like serotonin and dopamine.

③ Food shortages and encountering predators put people under more severe stress compared to the pandemic.

④ The brain mechanism that is activated in stressful situations may lead to unhealthy habits.

問7 空所(オ)に入れるべき最も適切な語を①～④の中から1つ選びなさい。

① high-calorie   ② sweet-and-sour

③ ready-made   ④ self-regulated

問8 下線部(カ)In a nutshell の言い換えとして最も適切な表現を①～④の中から1つ選びなさい。

① To some extent   ② In concert

③ In short   ④ In the long run

問9 第 10 段落〜第 12 段落 (Many people find ... its unwanted consequences.)
の内容と一致する文を①〜④の中から 1 つ選びなさい。

① When we eat calorie-dense food, we might feel happier than before,
but the feeling doesn't last long.

② When the signals traveling through the vagus nerve increase, people
sometimes lose their appetite.

③ Whether people gain or lose weight is not related to any brain
mechanisms.

④ Extra stress from the pandemic combined with plenty of distractions
at home was the main cause of unwanted weight change.

問10 本文に書かれている内容と一致するものを①〜④の中から 1 つ選びなさ
い。

① Under an extremely stressful situation, it is more likely that people
will stop eating rather than overeat.

② To avoid the undesired consequences of stressful situations, we
should try alternative methods of reducing stress such as positive
self-talk.

③ The fight-or-flight response has not played a major role in causing
undesired weight change over the pandemic.

④ When you need to control your weight, you should turn on your
fight-or-flight response by stressing yourself out.

次の英文を読んで，あとの問いに答えなさい。

The art of persuasion is one of the most important business skills. Without the ability to persuade others to support your ideas, you won't be able to obtain the support you need (ア)to turn those ideas into realities. And though most people are unaware of it, the ways you seek to persuade others and the kinds of arguments you find persuasive are deeply rooted in your cultural ideas and attitudes. Far (イ) being universal, the art of persuasion is one that is profoundly culture-based.

(ウ)That was the hard lesson learned by Kara Williams, an American engineer newly employed as a research manager for a German automobile firm. As one of the leading experts in her field, Williams had extensive experience presenting recommendations and influencing her American colleagues to follow her ideas. But when Williams began working in a German environment, she didn't realize that being persuasive would require a different approach. "When I think back to my first presentation to my new German bosses, (エ)I wish I had understood the difference and hadn't let their feedback get under my skin. If I had been cool enough I might have been able to save the situation."

Williams' first project was providing technical advice on how to reduce carbon emissions* from one of the group's "green" car models. After visiting several automobile plants, observing the systems and processes there, and meeting with dozens of experts and users, Williams developed a set of recommendations (オ)that she felt would meet the company's goals. She traveled to Munich* to give a one-hour presentation to the decision makers — a group of German directors.

"It was my first presentation, and its success would be important for my reputation," Williams recalls. In preparation for the meeting, Williams thought carefully about (力) to give the most persuasive presentation, practicing her arguments, anticipating questions that might arise, and preparing responses to those questions.

Williams delivered her presentation in a small hall with the directors seated in rows of chairs. She began by getting right to the point, explaining the strategies she would recommend based on her findings. But before she had finished with the first part, one of the directors raised his hand and protested, "How did you get to these conclusions? You are giving us your recommendations, but I don't understand how you got here. How many people did you interview? What questions did you ask?"

Then another director jumped in: "Please explain what methods you used for analyzing your data and how that led you to come to these findings."

"I was shocked," Williams remembers. "I assured them that the methods behind my recommendations were sound, but the questions and challenges continued. The more they questioned me, the more I got the feeling that they were attacking my research ability, (ﾁ)which puzzled and annoyed me. I am an experienced specialist in engineering with a lot of know-how that is widely acknowledged. Their effort to test my conclusions, I felt, showed a real lack of respect. (ク)What rudeness to think that they would be better able to judge than I am!"

Williams reacted defensively, and the presentation began collapsing from there. "(ケ)I kick myself now for having allowed their approach to run me off my point," she says. "Needless to say, they did not approve my recommendations, and three months of research time (コ)<u>went down the drain</u>."

The stone wall Williams ran into illustrates the hard truth that our ability to persuade others depends not only on the strength of our message but on how we build our arguments and the persuasive techniques we employ.

＊carbon emissions：炭素排出量
　Munich：ミュンヘン（ドイツ南部の都市）

問1 下線部（ア）と同じ用法で使われているものを，次の①～⑤の中から1つ選びなさい。

① Not a soul was <u>to be</u> seen in the street.

② Give me something cold <u>to drink</u>.

③ I really would like <u>to visit</u> Hawaii.

④ <u>To tell</u> you the truth, I don't like carrots.

⑤ More training is essential <u>to get</u> a gold medal.

問2 空所（イ）へ入れるのに最もふさわしいものを，次の①～⑤の中から1つ選びなさい。

① away　　② from　　③ with　　④ as　　⑤ off

問3 下線部(ウ)の内容として最もふさわしいものを，次の①〜⑤の中から1つ選びなさい。

① 説得術の重要性に気づいていない人が多い。

② 説得術は，国語教育の重要な問題だ。

③ 説得術は，文化に深く根差している。

④ 他人を説得しようと思えば，根拠が必要だ。

⑤ 説得術がなければ，出世できない。

問4 下線部(エ)の内容として最もふさわしいものを，次の①〜⑤の中から1つ選びなさい。

① アプローチに違いがあったとしても，あの反応は無視してはいけなかった。

② アプローチの違いを理解して，あの人たちの反応にいらだたなければよかったのになあ。

③ アプローチの違いを理解してさえいれば，あの人たちの反応を利用できたのに。

④ アプローチの違いをどれほど理解したところで，イライラは募ったであろう。

⑤ 私の望みは，別のアプローチを考えだして，彼らの反応を封じ込めることだった。

問5 下線部(オ)と同じ用法で使われているものを，次の①〜⑤の中から1つ選びなさい。

① It seems that she is a native speaker of French.

② She is very happy that you arrived here safe and sound.

③ He must be crazy that he spent all his money on used clothes.

④ Study harder so that you may pass the exam.

⑤ Lend me a book that will tell me how to grow roses.

問6 空所(カ)へ入れるのに最もふさわしいものを，次の①〜⑤の中から1つ選びなさい。

① how ② when ③ why ④ which ⑤ where

問7 下線部(キ)の内容として最もふさわしいものを，次の①〜⑤の中から1つ選びなさい。

① 私が薦めた改善内容

② 私のとった調査方法

③ 彼らがどんどん質問しないこと

④ 私の調査能力

⑤ 私の調査能力が攻撃されていると感じたこと

問8 下線部(**ク**)の意味として最もふさわしいものを，次の①〜⑤の中から１つ選びなさい。

① この私よりも彼らの方が判断力があると思うなんて，なんて失礼なのだ。

② あの人たちの私に対する判断の根拠は，いったいどこにあるというのだ。

③ 彼らの方が私自身よりも判断力があると思うと，なんと情けなく思われることか。

④ 彼らの方が私よりも優れた判断をしているとは，まったく信じがたい。

⑤ 人よりも優れた判断をするためには，どんな不作法も許されるのだ。

問9 下線部(**ケ**)の内容として最もふさわしいものを，次の①〜⑤の中から１つ選びなさい。

① 今では，なぜ彼らのやり方を利用して要点を主張しなかったのか，後悔している。

② 私は自分を叱咤激励しながら，私の主張する要点の取り組みを進めるつもりだ。

③ 彼らのペースにはまって，思うような主張ができなかったのが嘆かわしい。

④ 床を蹴っている自分の姿が嘆かわしくて，つい話のポイントがずれてしまった。

⑤ 質問攻めによって脱線してしまったが，今ではそれが励みになっている。

問10 下線部(コ)の言い換えとして最もふさわしいものを，次の①〜⑤の中から1つ選びなさい。

① was rewarded　　② was wasted　　③ was fruitful
④ was quite useful　　⑤ got downsized

問11 本文の内容に合致するものを，次の①〜⑦の中から2つ選びなさい。

① 説得術は，ビジネスにおいては必ずしも重要ではない。

② Kara Williams は，ドイツの自動車会社から派遣されてアメリカ企業に来た。

③ Kara Williams は，ドイツでのプレゼンテーションのためにたくさんの専門家や消費者に会った。

④ Kara Williams は，ドイツでのプレゼンテーションで，前置きをたっぷりとって話した。

⑤ 会社の重役たちは，プレゼンテーションが終わったとたん，矢継ぎ早に質問しだした。

⑥ Kara Williams は，防御を固めたプレゼンテーションによって成功をおさめた。

⑦ 説得力は，伝えるメッセージの強さばかりでなく，議論の筋道と説得の仕方にかかっている。

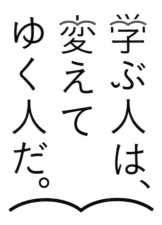

学ぶ人は、
変えて
ゆく人だ。

目の前にある問題はもちろん、

人生の問いや、

社会の課題を自ら見つけ、

挑み続けるために、人は学ぶ。

「学び」で、

少しずつ世界は変えてゆける。

いつでも、どこでも、誰でも、

学ぶことができる世の中へ。

旺文社

英語長文

駿台予備学校講師 三浦淳一 著

3 私大標準レベル

三訂版

はじめに

　大学受験に向けた英語学習は，書店の学習参考書コーナーに行けばすぐにわかるとおり，とても細分化されています。単語・熟語，文法・語法，構文，英作文，長文読解，リスニング，会話表現，発音・アクセント…

　これを1つずつやっていたら，何年かかっても終わりそうにありません。

　「一石二鳥」という言葉がありますが，短期間で英語の学習を仕上げるには，いわば「一石五鳥」「一石六鳥」の学習をすることです。つまり，1つの学習で複数の効果を得られるような学習をすべきなのです。

　『大学入試 全レベル問題集　英語長文』シリーズは，長文読解の問題集という形をとっていますが，これにとどまらず，語彙力をつけたり，重要な文法事項の確認をしたり，音声を用いた学習により，発音・アクセント，リスニングの力をつけることも目指しています。

　本シリーズはレベル別に6段階で構成されており，必ず自分にピッタリ合った1冊があるはずです。また，現時点の実力と志望校のレベルにギャップがあるなら，1～2段階レベルを下げて，英語力を基礎から鍛え直すのもおすすめです。受験生はもちろん，高校1・2年生からスタートすることもできます。

　本シリーズは最新の大学入試問題の傾向に対応し，さらに，英語4技能（Reading / Listening / Writing / Speaking）を今後ますます重視する入試制度にも対応しうる，本質的・普遍的な英語力をつけることを目的にしています。

　本シリーズを利用して，皆さんが第一志望の大学に合格することはもちろん，その先，一生の武器となる確固たる英語力を身につけてほしいと願っています。

三浦　淳一

目　次

音声について

本書の英文を読み上げた音声を，専用ウェブサイト・スマートフォンアプリで聞くことができます。英文ごとに，2種類の音声を収録しています。全文通し読みの音声と，段落ごとに区切ったややゆっくりめの音声があります。段落ごとに区切った音声は，ディクテーションでご利用ください。🔊 01 のように示しています。

●ウェブサイトで聞く方法
・以下のサイトにアクセスし，パスワードを入力してください。
　https://service.obunsha.co.jp/tokuten/zlr3/
　※すべて半角英数字。検索エンジンの「検索欄」は不可。
　パスワード：zlr3t

●スマートフォンアプリで聞く方法
・音声をスマートフォンアプリ「英語の友」で聞くことができます。「英語の友」で検索するか，右の二次元コードからアクセスしてください。
・パスワードを求められたら，上と同じパスワードを入力してください。

※ご注意ください　◆音声を再生する際の通信料にご注意ください。◆音声は MP3 形式となっています。音声の再生には MP3 を再生できる機器などが別途必要です。デジタルオーディオプレーヤーなどの機器への音声ファイルの転送方法は，各製品の取り扱い説明書などをご覧ください。ご使用機器，音声再生ソフトなどに関する技術的なご質問は，ハードメーカーもしくはソフトメーカーにお問い合わせください。◆スマートフォンやタブレットでは音声をダウンロードできないことがあります。◆本サービスは予告なく終了することがあります。

本シリーズの特長

「大学入試 全レベル問題集 英語長文」シリーズには, 以下の特長があります。

1. 細かく分かれたレベル設定

本シリーズはレベル別からなる6冊で構成されており, 学習者の皆さんそれぞれがベストな1冊を選んで大学入試対策をスタートできるようにしています。各書がレベルに応じた収録英文数と設問構成になっています。

2. 語彙力を重視

語彙力は語学学習における基本です。単語がわからなければ英文を読むにも書くにも不自由します。本書ではオールラウンドな語彙力をつけられるよう, 幅広いテーマの英文を選びました。各ユニットの最後に, 本文の単熟語や英文が復習できる確認問題や, 音声を利用した単語のディクテーション問題を設け, 語彙力が増強できるよう工夫しています。

3. 英文構造の明示

すべての英文の構造を示し（ＳＶＯＣ分析）, 英文を完全に理解できるようにしました。さらに, 本文の和訳例も, あまり意訳をせず, 文構造を反映させた直訳に近い日本語にしました。

4. 文法事項のわかりやすい解説

近年の入試問題では, 難関大学を中心に文法問題の出題が減少しており, 「文法問題を解くための文法学習」は, もはや時代遅れです。本書では「英文を正しく読むための文法」を心がけて解説しています。

5. 設問の的確な解説

すべての設問に, なるべく短く的確な解説をつけました。特に本文の内容に関する設問は, 根拠となる箇所を明示して解説しています。類書と比較しても, わかりやすく論理的な解説にしています。これは, 解説を読んで納得してほしいということもありますが, それ以上に, 読者の皆さんが自分で問題を解くときにも, このように論理的に考えて, 正解を導き出せるようになってほしいからです。

6. 音声による学習

付属の音声には本書に掲載した英文の音声が2パターンで収録されています。主にリスニング力UPを目的としたナチュラルに近いスピードのものは, シャドーイング*1 やオーバーラッピング*2 用です。また1つ1つの単語の発音がわかるようなややゆっくりしたスピードのものは, ディクテーション問題用です。

> *1 シャドーイング・・・すぐ後から音声を追いかけて, 同じ内容を口に出す練習方法
> *2 オーバーラッピング・・・流れてくる音声とぴったり重なるように口に出す練習方法

著者紹介：**三浦淳一**（みうら じゅんいち）

早稲田大学文学部卒。現在, 駿台予備学校・医学部受験専門予備校 YMS 講師。『全国人学入試問題正解 英語』（旺文社）解答・解説執筆者。『入門 英語長文問題精講 [3 訂版]』『医学部の英語』『大学入学共通テスト 英語 [リーディング] 集中講義』（以上, 旺文社）, 『世界一覚えやすい中学英語の基本文例 100』（以上, KADOKAWA）ほか著書多数。「N 予備校」「学びエイド」などで映像授業も担当する。

〔協力各氏・各社〕

装丁デザイン：ライトパブリシティ	録 音・編 集：ユニバ合同会社
本文デザイン：イイタカデザイン	ナレーション：Ann Slater, Guy Perryman, Katie Adler
校　　　正：笠井嘉雄(e.editors), 入江 泉, 山本知子,	編 集 協 力：株式会社オルタナプロ
Jason A. Chau	編 集 担 当：上原 英

志望校レベルと「全レベル問題集 英語長文」シリーズのレベル対応表

* 掲載の大学名は購入していただく際の目安です。また, 大学名は刊行時のものです。

本書のレベル	各レベルの該当大学
① 基礎レベル	高校基礎～大学受験準備
② 共通テストレベル	共通テストレベル
③ 私大標準レベル	日本大学・東洋大学・駒澤大学・専修大学・京都産業大学・近畿大学・甲南大学・龍谷大学・札幌大学・亜細亜大学・國學院大學・東京電機大学・武蔵大学・神奈川大学・愛知大学・東海大学・名城大学・追手門学院大学・神戸学院大学・広島国際大学・松山大学・福岡大学 他
④ 私大上位レベル	学習院大学・明治大学・青山学院大学・立教大学・中央大学・法政大学・芝浦工業大学・成城大学・成蹊大学・津田塾大学・東京理科大学・日本女子大学・明治学院大学・獨協大学・北里大学・南山大学・関西外国語大学・西南学院大学 他
⑤ 私大最難関レベル	早稲田大学・慶應義塾大学・上智大学・関西大学・関西学院大学・同志社大学・立命館大学 他
⑥ 国公立大レベル	北海道大学・東北大学・東京大学・一橋大学・東京工業大学・名古屋大学・京都大学・大阪大学・神戸大学・広島大学・九州大学 他

本書で使用している記号一覧

🚫 Check! ············· 文法事項の説明

🔊 ············· 音声番号

SVOC分析

S, V, O, C ········ 主節における文の要素

S, V, O, C ········ 従属節における文の要素

S′, V′, O′, C′ ······ 意味上の関係

① ② ③ ··········· 並列関係にある要素

〈　　〉··········· 名詞句, 名詞節

〔　　〕··········· 形容詞句, 形容詞節

（　　）··········· 副詞句, 副詞節

関代 ·············· 関係代名詞

関副 ·············· 関係副詞

等接 ·············· 等位接続詞

従接 ·············· 従属接続詞

疑 ················ 疑問詞

…so ～ that … 相関語句

語句リスト

動 ················· 動詞

名 ················· 名詞

形 ················· 形容詞

副 ················· 副詞

接 ················· 接続詞

前 ················· 前置詞

熟 ················· 熟語

志望大学別 入試長文分析と学習アドバイス

大学名	日本大学	東洋大学	駒澤大学
英文レベル※	★2.0 1······2······3······4	★2.0 1······2······3······4	★1.9 1······2······3······4
出題ジャンル	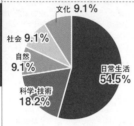文化 9.1% 社会 9.1% 自然 9.1% 科学・技術 18.2% 日常生活 54.5%	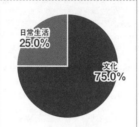日常生活 25.0% 文化 75.0%	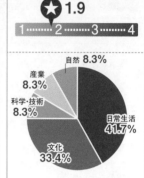自然 8.3% 産業 8.3% 科学・技術 8.3% 文化 33.4% 日常生活 41.7%
	長文問題の平均出題大問数 **3.7 問**	長文問題の平均出題大問数 **2.0 問**	長文問題の平均出題大問数 **3.0 問**
	長文1題あたり平均語数 **375 語**	長文1題あたり平均語数 **551 語**	長文1題あたり平均語数 **319 語**
設問形式	☑ 内容一致（選択式） ☐ 内容一致（T or F） ☑ 空所補充 ☐ 下線部言い換え ☑ 表題選択 ☐ 下線部和訳 ☐ 記述説明 ☑ その他	☑ 内容一致（選択式） ☑ 内容一致（T or F） ☑ 空所補充 ☑ 下線部言い換え ☑ 表題選択 ☐ 下線部和訳 ☐ 記述説明 ☑ その他	☑ 内容一致（選択式） ☐ 内容一致（T or F） ☑ 空所補充 ☑ 下線部言い換え ☑ 表題選択 ☐ 下線部和訳 ☐ 記述説明 ☐ その他
三浦先生Check!	基本的に記述問題は出題されない。長文読解の大問は3つで、それぞれ内容一致問題、空所補充問題、文中での語句整序問題となっている。	空所補充は文法的な理解を問うもの。内容真偽判定問題が中心。日常生活や文化など、わかりやすいテーマの文章が多い。	英文は短めであり、設問は内容一致問題が中心で、取り組みやすい。近年は図表など資料と関連付けた英文が出題されている。

※T or F：内容真偽判定問題

6

専修大学

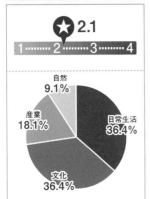

★2.1

1 ⋯⋯⋯ 2 ⋯⋯⋯ 3 ⋯⋯⋯ 4

自然
9.1%

産業
18.1%

日常生活
36.4%

文化
36.4%

長文問題の平均出題大問数
2.8 問

長文1題あたり平均語数
574 語

- ☑ 内容一致（選択式）
- ☐ 内容一致（T or F）
- ☑ 空所補充
- ☑ 下線部言い換え
- ☑ 表題選択
- ☐ 下線部和訳
- ☐ 記述説明
- ☑ その他

難解な語句が含まれる英文を出すが，語注が多いので理解の妨げにはならない。内容一致問題は選択肢が日本語なので解きやすい。

京都産業大学

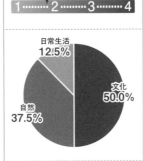

★1.9

1 ⋯⋯⋯ 2 ⋯⋯⋯ 3 ⋯⋯⋯ 4

日常生活
12.5%

文化
50.0%

自然
37.5%

長文問題の平均出題大問数
2.0 問

長文1題あたり平均語数
386 語

- ☑ 内容一致（選択式）
- ☐ 内容一致（T or F）
- ☑ 空所補充
- ☐ 下線部言い換え
- ☑ 表題選択
- ☐ 下線部和訳
- ☐ 記述説明
- ☐ その他

空所補充と内容一致中心のシンプルな出題形式。内容一致問題は事前に設問に目を通すことがポイント。英文の内容は具体的でわかりやすい。

近畿大学

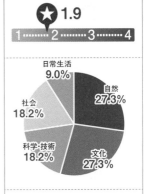

★1.9

1 ⋯⋯⋯ 2 ⋯⋯⋯ 3 ⋯⋯⋯ 4

日常生活
9.0%

自然
27.3%

社会
18.2%

科学・技術
18.2%

文化
27.3%

長文問題の平均出題大問数
2.0 問

長文1題あたり平均語数
282 語

- ☑ 内容一致（選択式）
- ☐ 内容一致（T or F）
- ☑ 空所補充
- ☑ 下線部言い換え
- ☐ 表題選択
- ☐ 下線部和訳
- ☐ 記述説明
- ☐ その他

短めの英文＋空所補充問題，長めの英文＋内容一致問題という構成。内容一致問題は段落ごとの理解を問う設問が中心となる。

大学名	甲南大学	龍谷大学	札幌大学
英文レベル*	★2.0 1……2……3……4	★2.0 1……2……3……4	★2.0 1……2……3……4
出題ジャンル	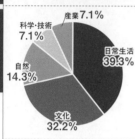産業7.1% 科学・技術 7.1% 日常生活 39.3% 自然 14.3% 文化 32.2%	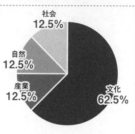社会 12.5% 自然 12.5% 産業 12.5% 文化 62.5%	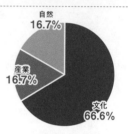自然 16.7% 産業 16.7% 文化 66.6%
	長文問題の平均出題大問数 **3.8 問**	長文問題の平均出題大問数 **2.0 問**	長文問題の平均出題大問数 **2.0 問**
	長文1題あたり平均語数 **424 語**	長文1題あたり平均語数 **596 語**	長文1題あたり平均語数 **593 語**
設問形式	☑内容一致（選択式） ☐内容一致（T or F） ☑空所補充 ☑下線部言い換え ☐表題選択 ☑下線部和訳 ☐記述説明 ☑その他	☑内容一致（選択式） ☐内容一致（T or F） ☑空所補充 ☑下線部言い換え ☑表題選択 ☐下線部和訳 ☐記述説明 ☐その他	☐内容一致（選択式） ☑内容一致（T or F） ☑空所補充 ☐下線部言い換え ☐表題選択 ☑下線部和訳 ☑記述説明 ☑その他
三浦先生Check!	内容一致問題は段落ごとの理解を問う問題が中心。他は単語・熟語の知識問題など，細かい小問が多数。文系学部には下線部和訳問題がある。	文中に多くの下線があり，細かく理解を問う。特定の段落の内容を問う問題もあるので，読み進めながら段落ごとに設問を処理するのが効率的。	下線部和訳問題や記述説明問題などが出題され，記述力が問われる。T or F 型の内容真偽問題が特徴的。

※T or F：内容真偽判定問題

亜細亜大学

★1.8

1┄┄┄2┄┄┄3┄┄┄4

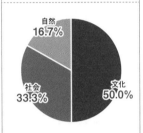

自然
16.7%

社会
33.3%

文化
50.0%

長文問題の平均出題大問数
2.0 問

長文1題あたり平均語数
660 語

- ✓ 内容一致（選択式）
- ☐ 内容一致（T or F）
- ✓ 空所補充
- ☐ 下線部言い換え
- ☐ 表題選択
- ☐ 下線部和訳
- ☐ 記述説明
- ☐ その他

長文読解は大問２つで，それぞれ空所補充問題と内容一致問題。内容一致問題は，英文を段落ごとに区切って内容を問う形式が特徴的。

神奈川大学

★1.9

1┄┄┄2┄┄┄3┄┄┄4

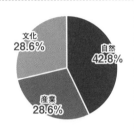

文化
28.6%

自然
42.8%

産業
28.6%

長文問題の平均出題大問数
2.0 問

長文1題あたり平均語数
555 語

- ✓ 内容一致（選択式）
- ☐ 内容一致（T or F）
- ☐ 空所補充
- ✓ 下線部言い換え
- ☐ 表題選択
- ☐ 下線部和訳
- ☐ 記述説明
- ☐ その他

基本的に下線部言い換えと内容一致のみ。必修単語にも注が付いている。内容一致問題はあらかじめ問いに目を通しておくと効果的。

東京経済大学

★1.9

1┄┄┄2┄┄┄3┄┄┄4

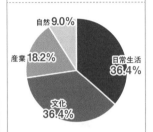

自然 9.0%

産業 18.2%

日常生活
36.4%

文化
36.4%

長文問題の平均出題大問数
3.0 問

長文1題あたり平均語数
493 語

- ✓ 内容一致（選択式）
- ☐ 内容一致（T or F）
- ✓ 空所補充
- ✓ 下線部言い換え
- ✓ 表題選択
- ☐ 下線部和訳
- ☐ 記述説明
- ☐ その他

長文読解は大問３つで，うち２つは内容一致，１つは空所補充が中心。前者は１～２段落読むごとに設問をチェックすると効率的。

大学名	愛知大学	中京大学	名城大学
英文レベル※	 ★2.0　1……2……3……4	 ★2.3　1……2……3……4	 ★1.9　1……2……3……4
出題ジャンル	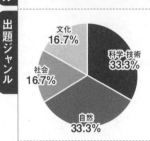 文化 16.7%／科学・技術 33.3%／社会 16.7%／自然 33.3%	 文化 16.7%／社会 33.3%／自然 16.7%／日常生活 33.3%	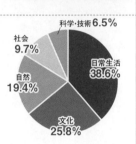 科学・技術 6.5%／社会 9.7%／自然 19.4%／日常生活 38.6%／文化 25.8%
	長文問題の平均出題大問数 **2.0 問**	長文問題の平均出題大問数 **3.0 問**	長文問題の平均出題大問数 **2.4 問**
	長文1題あたり平均語数 **660 語**	長文1題あたり平均語数 **282 語**	長文1題あたり平均語数 **565 語**
設問形式	☑ 内容一致（選択式） ☐ 内容一致（T or F） ☑ 空所補充 ☑ 下線部言い換え ☑ 表題選択 ☑ 下線部和訳 ☑ 記述説明 ☑ その他	☑ 内容一致（選択式） ☐ 内容一致（T or F） ☑ 空所補充 ☑ 下線部言い換え ☐ 表題選択 ☐ 下線部和訳 ☐ 記述説明 ☐ その他	☑ 内容一致（選択式） ☐ 内容一致（T or F） ☑ 空所補充 ☑ 下線部言い換え ☑ 表題選択 ☑ 下線部和訳 ☑ 記述説明 ☑ その他
三浦先生Check!	大問2つの中に含まれる小問の数が非常に多く，指示語，用法識別，語句整序など多岐にわたる。記述問題は，派生語を書かせる問題や下線部和訳など。	空所補充，内容一致，下線部言い換え問題がバランス良く出題される。毎年出題されているグラフを含む問題は慣れが必要。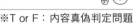	内容一致問題が中心で，図表などの資料と関連付けた英文も出題される。一部の学部では下線部和訳問題や記述説明問題なども。

※T or F：内容真偽判定問題

追手門学院大学

⭐ **2.0**

1 ---- 2 ---- 3 ---- 4

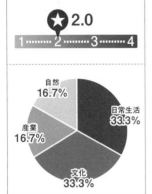

長文問題の平均出題大問数

2.0 問

長文1題あたり平均語数

506 語

- ☑ 内容一致（選択式）
- ☐ 内容一致（T or F）
- ☑ 空所補充
- ☑ 下線部言い換え
- ☑ 表題選択
- ☐ 下線部和訳
- ☐ 記述説明
- ☐ その他

読解問題は大問２つ。内容一致と空所補充が中心で，各大問に表題選択問題が含まれる。英文は平易であり，内容一致問題は全問正解を狙える。

神戸学院大学

⭐ **1.9**

1 ---- 2 ---- 3 ---- 4

長文問題の平均出題大問数

2.5 問

長文1題あたり平均語数

424 語

- ☑ 内容一致（選択式）
- ☐ 内容一致（T or F）
- ☑ 空所補充
- ☑ 下線部言い換え
- ☐ 表題選択
- ☐ 下線部和訳
- ☐ 記述説明
- ☑ その他

出題形式は内容一致が中心で，他に空所補充，下線部言い換えなど。「正しくないもの」を選ばせる問題に注意。要約文を完成させる問題が特徴的。

掲載データは，『2021年受験用 全国大学入試問題正解 英語』〜『2024年〃』を独自に分析したものです（一部，問題非公開の大学・学部については対象分析年度が異なる場合があります）。

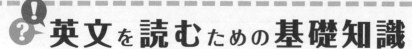

英文を読むための基礎知識

英文を読む上で，単語や熟語の知識が必要なのは当然である。しかし，語句の意味がわかれば英文を正しく理解できるというわけではない。英文は日本語とは異なる「構造」を持っているので，「構造」を把握することが英文を読むときには不可欠だ。

文型と文の要素

(1) 文型とは，英語の文のパターンを分類したものだ。英語の文には5つの文型がある。

第1文型：**S ＋ V**
第2文型：**S ＋ V ＋ C**
第3文型：**S ＋ V ＋ O**
第4文型：**S ＋ V ＋ O ＋ O**
第5文型：**S ＋ V ＋ O ＋ C**

(2) そして，文型を構成する1つ1つのパーツのことを，文の要素と呼んでいる。これも5つある。

S（主語）：「～は」「～が」と訳す。**名詞**。
V（述語）：「～する」「～である」と訳す。**動詞**。
O（目的語）：「～を」「～に」と訳す。**名詞**。
C（補語）：決まった訳し方はない。**名詞**または**形容詞**。
M（修飾語）：決まった訳し方はない。**形容詞**または**副詞**。

句と節

「句」も「節」も，2語以上のカタマリを意味するが，以下のような違いがある。

「句」→〈S＋V〉を含まないカタマリ　　「節」→〈S＋V〉を含むカタマリ

1. 句

(1) 名詞句

S, O, C になる句。**不定詞や動名詞のカタマリ**である。どちらも，「～すること」と訳す場合が多い。

例　My desire is 〈to study abroad〉.　　「私の希望は留学することだ」
　　S　　　　V　C

(2) 形容詞句

名詞を修飾する句。**不定詞，分詞，前置詞のカタマリ**がこれにあたる。

例　I have a lot of *homework* [to do].　　「私にはやるべき宿題がたくさんある」
　　S　V　　　　　O

(3) 副詞句

名詞以外（主に動詞）を修飾する句。**不定詞，分詞，前置詞のカタマリ**がこれにあたる。なお，分詞が副詞句を作ると，「分詞構文」と呼ばれ，【時】【理由】【付帯状況】などの意味を表す。

例　He *went* to America 〈to study jazz〉.　　「彼はジャズの研究をするためにアメリカへ行った」
　　S　V

to study jazz という不定詞のカタマリが went という動詞を修飾している。【目的】「～するために」

例　He *entered* the room,（taking off his hat）.　「彼は帽子を脱ぎながら部屋に入った」
　　S　　V　　　O

taking off his hat という分詞のカタマリ（分詞構文）が entered という動詞を修飾している。
【付帯状況】「～しながら」

例　I *got*（to the station）（at ten）.　　「私は10時に駅に到着した」
　　S　V

to the station と at ten という2つの前置詞のカタマリが，いずれも got という動詞を修飾している。

2. 節

(1) 名詞節

S, O, C になる節。①従属接続詞 (that / if / whether),②疑問詞,③関係詞が名詞節を作る。

① 従属接続詞とは,節を作るタイプの接続詞のこと。従属接続詞は数多くあるが,その中で**名詞節を作るの**は **that**「…こと」／ **if**「…かどうか」／ **whether**「…かどうか」の3つだけで,それ以外のすべての従属接続詞は副詞節しか作れない。

例　〈**That** you study Spanish now〉is a good idea.

「あなたが今スペイン語を勉強する**こと**はいい考えだ」

例　I don't know 〈**if**[**whether**] he will come here tomorrow〉.

「明日彼がここに来るの**かどうか**わからない」

② 疑問詞も名詞節を作る。

例　I don't know 〈**what** he wants〉.　「私は,彼が**何を**欲しがっているの**か**知らない」

③ **一部の関係詞も名詞節を作る**ことがある。これは,関係詞の中では少数派であり,関係詞の大半は,次に述べる形容詞節を作る。名詞節を作る関係詞は,**what**「…すること／…するもの」と**how**「…する方法」を押さえておこう。

例　〈**What** I want〉is a new car.　「私が欲しい**もの**は新しい車だ」

例　This is 〈**how** I solved the problem〉.

「これが,私が問題を解決した**方法**だ (→このようにして私は問題を解決した)」

(2) 形容詞節

名詞を修飾する働きをする節。これを作るのは**関係詞だけ**だ。

例　I have *a friend* 〔**who** lives in Osaka〕.　「私には大阪に住んでいる友人がいる」

関係代名詞 who から始まるカタマリが a friend という名詞を修飾。

例　This is *the place* 〔**where** I met her first〕.「ここは私が初めて彼女に会った場所だ」

関係副詞 where から始まるカタマリが the place という名詞を修飾。

(3) 副詞節

名詞以外 (主に動詞) を修飾する節。従属接続詞はすべて,副詞節を作ることができる。

例　I like him (**because** he is generous).　「彼は気前がいいので,私は彼が好きだ」

従属接続詞 because から始まるカタマリが like という動詞を修飾している。

＊ 上の名詞節のところで出てきた that / if / whether は,名詞節だけではなく副詞節も作ることができる (ただし,that は so ～ that … 構文など,特殊な構文に限られる)。if は「もし…すれば」,whether は「…であろうとなかろうと」の意味では副詞節である。

例　I will stay home (**if** it rains tomorrow).　「もし明日雨が降ったら,私は家にいるつもりだ」

従属接続詞 if から始まるカタマリが stay という動詞を修飾している。

このほか,「複合関係詞」と呼ばれる特殊な関係詞が副詞節を作ることができる。

例　I will reject your offer (**whatever** you say).「たとえ君が何を言っても,私は君の申し出を断ります」

※ さらに詳しい解説は,本シリーズのレベル①(p.6～15),レベル②(p.6～19)を参照して下さい。

解答

解 説

問

(ア)【存在】を表す with。**with the exception of ～** で「**～を例外として，～という例外はあるが**」の意味。

(イ) ① **wherever**「どこに…しても」が文意に合う。② however「どんなに［どのように］…しても」は文意に合わない。③ whenever については，文末に at the end of the day という時を表す語句があるので whenever「いつ…しても」では矛盾がある。④ whoever は後に不完全な文(SやOの欠けた文)が続くので文法的に不可。

(ウ) **the same ～ as S+V** で「**S が V するのと同じ～**」の意味。

(エ) ① for は等位接続詞で「というのは…だからだ」の意味があるが，ここでは前後に因果関係はないので不可。② that は接続詞の場合，名詞節を導いて「…ということ」の意味だが，ここでは空所以下がなくても文が成立する(OやCなどの名詞要素の欠落はない)ことから，名詞節とは考えられない。③ unless は「…しない限り」の意味で副詞節を導くが，意味的に不可。④ **while** は【時】【譲歩】【対比】の意味を持ち，ここでは「…する間」が文意に合う。

(オ)「火を使って」の意味で【付帯状況】を表す分詞構文と考え，現在分詞の③ Using を選ぶ。① Use だと原形なので命令文になるが，この後に接続詞がなく S+V が続いているので不可。② To use だと「火を使うために」と【目的】の意味になるが，内容として不自然。④ Used は分詞構文で【受動】を表す過去分詞と考えれば fire という O が続かないはずだし，過去形と考えても S がない点がおかしい。

第 1 段落　文の構造と語句のチェック

¹A vast stretch of land lies untouched (by civilization) (in the back country
　　S　　　　　　　V　　C

〔 of the eastern portion 〔 of the African continent 〕〕). ²(With the occasional

exception of a big-animal hunter), foreigners never enter this area. ³(Aside
　　　　　　　　　　　　　　　　S　　　　V　　O

from the Wandorobo tribe), even the natives stay away (from this particular
　　　　　　　　　　　　　　　　S　　　　V

area) (because it is the home 〔 of the deadly tsetse fly 〕). ⁴The tribe depend on
　　　　従接　S V　　C　　　　　　　　　　　　　　　　S　　　V

the forest (for their lives), ①(eating its roots and fruits) and ②(making
　O　　　　　　　　　　　　　　　　V′　　O′　　　等接　　V′

their homes (wherever they find themselves (at the end of the day))).
　O′　　　　従接　S　V　　O

┌── 関代 which 省略
⁵One of the things 〔 they usually eat 〕 is honey. ⁶They obtain it (through an
　S　　　　　　S　　　V　V　C　　S　　V　O

ancient, symbiotic relationship 〔 with a bird 〔 known as the Indicator 〕〕).

⁷The scientific community finally confirmed the report 〈 that this bird
　　　S　　　　　　V　　　　O　　従接（同格）　S

intentionally led the natives (to trees 〔 containing the honey of wild bees〕)〉.
　　　V　　O

⁸Other species of honey guides are also known (to take advantage of
　　　S　　　　　V　　　　V′

the search efforts of some animals (in much the same way 〔 as the Indicator
　O′　　　　　　　　　　　　　　　　　　　　　関代　S

15

$\underset{\text{V}}{\underline{\text{uses}}}\ \underset{\text{O}}{\underline{\text{men}}}$])).

訳 ¹アフリカ大陸東部の奥地に広大に広がる土地が，文明から手つかずの状態で残っている。²大型動物を求めるハンターという時折の例外はあるものの，外国人はこの地域にまったく入らない。³ワンドロボ族は別として，原住民でさえこの特別な地域には近づかない。なぜなら，そこは死をもたらすツェツェバエの生息地だからだ。⁴ワンドロボ族は生活を森林に依存しており，その根や果実を食べ，1日の終わりにはどこにいようとも，その場所に住処を作る。⁵彼らが普段食べるものの1つがハチミツである。⁶彼らは，インディケーター（指示する者）として知られる鳥との昔からの共生関係を通じてハチミツを手に入れる。⁷科学界はついに，この鳥が意図的に原住民を野生のミツバチのハチミツを含む樹木に案内しているという報告の裏付けをとった。⁸他の種のハチミツ案内役も，このインディケーターが人間を利用するのとほとんど同じ方法で，動物たちがハチミツを探す労力を利用していることが知られている。

Check! 第7文の The scientific community finally confirmed the report **that** this bird intentionally led the natives to trees containing the honey of wild bees. の that は【同格】の接続詞で，that 以下が直前の report の具体的内容を説明している。

語句

vast	形 広大な	**tribe**	名 部族
stretch	名 広がり，一帯	**native**	名 原住民，現地人
lie	動 〜のままである	**stay away from 〜**	
＊活用：lie-lay-lain			熟 〜に近づかない，〜を避ける
untouched	形 手つかずの，未開発の	**particular**	形 特別な
civilization	名 文明	home	名 生息地，住処
back country	名 奥地，僻地，未開地	**deadly**	形 死を招く
eastern	形 東の	**depend on A for B**	
portion	名 部分		熟 AにBを頼る，BのためにAに依存する
continent	名 大陸	**forest**	名 森林，山林
occasional	形 時々の	**root**	名 （植物の）根
exception	名 例外	**wherever**	接 どこで[に]…しても
hunter	名 ハンター，狩人	**at the end of 〜**	熟 〜の終わりに
foreigner	名 外国人	**honey**	名 ハチミツ
enter	動 入る	**obtain**	動 手に入れる
area	名 地域，地方	**ancient**	形 古い，昔からの
aside from 〜	熟 〜は別として，〜以外に	**relationship**	名 関係
		indicator	名 指示する者，指標，標識

scientific	形	科学の, 科学的な	**species**	名	(動植物の)種, 種類
community	名	共同体, ～界	**guide**	名	案内役, ガイド
confirm	動	確証する, 裏付ける	**take advantage of ～**	熟	～を利用する
intentionally	副	わざと, 意図的に	**search**	名	探求, 捜索
lead A to B	熟	A を B に導く, 案内する	**effort**	名	苦労, 作業, 活動, 努力
contain	動	含む	**much the same ～ as ...**		
wild	形	野生の		熟	…とほぼ同じ～
bee	名	ミツバチ			

第 2 段落　文の構造と語句のチェック

¹This amazing bird settles (in a tree 〔 near a Wandorobo camp 〕) and sings
　　　　S　　　　　　V①　　　　　　　　　　　　　　　　　　　　　　　　　　等接　V②

incessantly (until the men answer it (with whistles)). ²It then begins
　　　　　　　　従接　S　　V　　O　　　　　　　　　　　　　　　S　　　　　V

its leading flight. ³Singing, it hops (from tree to tree), (while the men continue
　　O　　　　　　　　　　　S　V　　　　　　　　　　　　　　従接　　S　　　V

their musical answering call). ⁴(When the bird reaches the tree), its voice
　　　　　O　　　　　　　　　　　　　　従接　　S　　V　　　O　　　　　S

becomes shriller and its followers examine the tree carefully. ⁵The Indicator
　V　　　C　　等接　　S　　　　　V　　　O　　　　　　　　　　　　　　S

usually sits (just over the bees' nests), and the men hear the sounds 〔 of the
　　　V　　　　　　　　　　　　　　　　　等接　S　　V　　　O

bees 〔 in the hollow trunk 〕〕. ⁶(Using fire), they smoke most of the bees (out of
　　　　　　　　　　　　　　　　　　V'　O'　S　　V　　　O

　　　　　　　the bees
　　　　　　　　‖
the tree), but those 〔 that escape the effects of the smoke 〕 attack the men
　　　　等接　S　　関代　V　　　　O　　　　　　　　　　V　　O

violently. ⁷(In spite of the attack), the Wandorobos gather the honey and leave
　　　　　　　　　　　　　　　　　　　　　S　　　　　V①　　O　　等接　V②

17

<u>a small gift</u> (for their bird guide).
    O

> 訳 ¹この驚くべき鳥はワンドロボ族の野営地の近くにある樹木に住みつき，人間が口笛で応答するまで絶え間なく鳴く。²そして，案内飛行を開始するのだ。³人間が音楽を奏でるように口笛で応答し続ける間，この鳥はさえずりながら木から木へと跳んで行く。⁴鳥が(ハチミツのとれる)木に着くと，声がさらに甲高くなり，後をつけてきた人間はその木を注意深く調べる。⁵インディケーターはたいていミツバチの巣の真上に止まり，そのとき人間には幹の空洞にいるミツバチの音が聞こえる。⁶火を利用して，人間はミツバチのほとんどを木からいぶし出すのだが，煙の影響を逃れたミツバチは人間に激しく攻撃を仕掛ける。⁷その攻撃にもかかわらず，ワンドロボ族はハチミツを集め，案内係の鳥に少々のプレゼントを残していくのである。

語 句

amazing	形 驚くべき，驚異的な
settle	動 定住する
camp	名 野営(地)
whistle	名 口笛
flight	名 飛ぶこと，飛行
hop	動 ぴょんぴょんと跳ぶ
follower	名 後をつける者
examine	動 調べる

nest	名 巣
smoke	動 いぶし出す，(煙で)追い出す
escape	動 逃れる，免れる
effect	名 影響
violently	副 激しく，乱暴に
in spite of ~	熟 ~にもかかわらず
gather	動 集める
leave	動 残す

文法事項の整理 ① 分詞構文

第 1 段落第 4 文の eating ... making ... についてみてみよう。

The tribe depend on the forest for their lives, **eating** its roots and fruits and **making** their homes wherever they find themselves at the end of the day.

　これは【分詞構文】で，分詞構文とは分詞（現在分詞，過去分詞）が副詞の働きをすることである。

　分詞構文は【時】【理由】【条件】【譲歩】など，様々な意味を表すことができる。

■分詞構文の表す意味

①【時】「〜するときに」

例 **Walking** across the street, I met an old friend of mine.
「道を歩いているときに私は旧友に会った」

②【理由】「〜するので」

例 **Written** in easy English, this book is suitable for beginners.
「易しい英語で書かれているので，この本は初心者に適している」

③【条件】「もし〜すれば」

例 **Born** in better days, he could have succeeded.
「もっといい時代に生まれていれば，彼は成功できたのだが」

④【譲歩】「〜だけれど」

例 **Admitting** what you say, I can't support you.
「あなたの言うことは認めるが，あなたを支援することはできない」

⑤【付帯状況】「〜しながら」

例 **Taking** off his hat, he entered the room.
「彼は帽子を脱ぎながら部屋に入った」

※分詞構文が文の後半（S＋Vより後）に出てくる場合は【付帯状況】を表すことが多い。「～しながら，～して，～したまま，そして～する」などと訳す。

> 例　He entered the room, **taking** off his hat.
> 「彼は帽子を脱ぎながら部屋に入った」
> 「彼は部屋に入り，そして帽子を脱いだ」

■第1段落第4文

The tribe depend on the forest for their lives, <u>eating</u> its roots and fruits and <u>making</u> their homes wherever they find themselves at the end of the day.

▶ eating と making が並列されており，いずれも【付帯状況】を表す分詞構文。「そして～する」などと訳す。

■第2段落第3文

<u>Singing</u>, it hops from tree to tree, while the men continue their musical answering call.

▶ Singing は現在分詞で，【付帯状況】を表す分詞構文。

■第2段落第6文

<u>Using</u> fire, they smoke most of the bees out of the tree, but those that escape the effects of the smoke attack the men violently.

▶ Using は現在分詞で，【付帯状況】を表す分詞構文。

確認問題

1. 次の和訳と対応する英語の語句を，頭文字を参考にして書き，空欄を完成させよう。

/40点

（各1点×20）

①	v				形	広大な
②	c				名	文明
③	c				名	大陸
④	e				名	例外
⑤	a	f	～		熟	～は別として，～以外に
⑥	s	a	f	～	熟	～に近づかない，～を避ける
⑦	o				動	手に入れる
⑧	a				形	古い，昔からの
⑨	i				名	指示する者，指標，標識
⑩	s				形	科学の，科学的な
⑪	i				副	わざと，意図的に
⑫	c				動	含む
⑬	s				名	(動植物の)種，種類
⑭	t	a	o	～	熟	～を利用する
⑮	a				形	驚くべき，驚異的な
⑯	s				動	定住する
⑰	n				名	巣
⑱	e				名	影響
⑲	v				副	激しく，乱暴に
⑳	i	s	o	～	熟	～にもかかわらず

2. 次の[ ]内の語句を並べ替えて，意味の通る英文を完成させよう。（各5点×2）

① A vast stretch [lies / by / land / untouched / civilization / of] in the back country of the eastern portion of the African continent.

② The scientific community finally confirmed the [that / bird / report / led / this / intentionally] the natives to trees containing the honey of wild bees.

3. 次の英文を和訳してみよう。(10点)

Using fire, they smoke most of the bees out of the tree, but those that escape the effects of the smoke attack the men violently.

＊smoke「いぶし出す．(煙で)追い出す」

ディクテーションしてみよう！

今回学習した英文に出てきた語句・表現を，＿＿＿に書き取ろう。

02
.
03

02 A vast stretch of land lies untouched by civilization in the back country of the eastern portion of the African continent. With ❶___
_____ a big-animal hunter, foreigners never enter this area. ❷_____ the Wandorobo tribe, even the natives stay away from this particular area because it is the home of the deadly tsetse fly. The tribe depend on the forest for their lives, eating its roots and fruits and making their homes wherever they find themselves at the end of the day. One of the things they usually eat is honey. They ❸_____ through an ancient, symbiotic relationship with a bird known as the Indicator. The scientific community finally confirmed the report that this bird ❹_____ the natives to trees containing the honey of wild bees. Other species of honey guides are also known to ❺_____ the search efforts of some animals in much the same way as the Indicator uses men.

03 ❻_____ settles in a tree near a Wandorobo camp and sings incessantly until the men answer it with whistles. It then begins its leading flight. Singing, it hops from tree to tree, while the men continue their musical answering call. When the bird

22

❼_____, its voice becomes shriller and its followers examine the tree carefully. The Indicator usually sits just over the bees' nests, and the men hear the sounds of the bees in the hollow trunk. Using fire, they smoke most of the bees out of the tree, but ❽_____ _____ the effects of the smoke attack the men violently. ❾_____ the attack, the Wandorobos gather the honey and leave a small gift for their bird guide.

確認問題の答 1. ① vast ② civilization ③ continent ④ exception
⑤ aside from ⑥ stay away from ⑦ obtain ⑧ ancient ⑨ indicator
⑩ scientific ⑪ intentionally ⑫ contain ⑬ species
⑭ take advantage of ⑮ amazing ⑯ settle ⑰ nest ⑱ effect
⑲ violently ⑳ in spite of

2. ① of land lies untouched by civilization （第1段落 第1文）
② report that this bird intentionally led （第1段落 第7文）

3. 火を利用して，人間はミツバチのほとんどを木からいぶし出すのだが，煙の影響を逃れたミツバチは人間に激しく攻撃を仕掛ける。 （第2段落 第6文）

ディクテーションしてみよう！の答 ❶ the occasional exception of ❷ Aside from
❸ obtain it ❹ intentionally led ❺ take advantage of ❻ This amazing bird
❼ reaches the tree ❽ those that escape ❾ In spite of

アドバイス ❶ exception の n と of の o がつながり，「ノブ」のように聞こえる（⇒連結）。
❽ those が複数名詞の代用，その後に関係代名詞の節が続くという文法的な理解がないと聞き取りは難しい。

2 解答・解説

解答

問1	②, ④, ⑤, ⑦, ⑧
問2	（ウ）the United Nations
	（エ）the International Committee for the Red Cross
問3	受賞者が資金調達を心配する必要なく仕事や研究を続けられるようにすること。
問4	（ア）アルフレッド・ノーベルは，ダイナマイトという強力な爆発物を発明した人物である。
	（イ）後に，1968年に，スウェーデン国立銀行が同行の創業300周年を記念して経済学の分野での賞を加えた。

解説

問1

① 「ノーベル賞はアルフレッド・ノーベルとともに働いた世界中の人々に与えられる」

▶ ノーベル賞受賞者の条件は第1段落第2文，第2段落第2文に記述があるが，「ノーベルとともに働いた」との内容は含まれていない。

② 「アルフレッド・ノーベルは発明家で，ノーベル賞を設立した」

▶ 第1段落第2文と一致。

③ 「1901年に6つのノーベル賞が初めて授与された」

▶ 第3段落第1文より，1901年には5部門のみ授与されたことがわかる。

④ 「経済学の分野での賞が後に加えられた」

▶ 第3段落第2文と一致。

⑤ 「ノーベル賞受賞者は現金を含む3つのものを与えられる」

▶ 第4段落第1文と一致。

⑥ 「金大中，大江健三郎，ネルソン・マンデラは皆，平和賞の受賞者である」

▶ 第5段落第2文により，大江健三郎は文学賞の受賞者とわかる。

⑦「**赤十字国際委員会はジャン・アンリ・デュナンによって創立された**」

▶ 最終段落第 2 文後半と一致。

⑧「**ジャン・アンリ・デュナンは 1901 年の第 1 回ノーベル賞受賞者の 1 人であった**」

▶ 最終段落第 2 文後半と一致。

問2

(ウ) ノーベル賞受賞者の団体は，第 5 段落第 2 文の the United Nations と，第 6 段落第 1 文の the International Committee for the Red Cross の 2 つが挙げられている。ここでは問題の指示に従い，下線部の含まれる第 5 段落にある the United Nations のみを答える。

(エ) this は原則として直前の文に指示内容がある。

問3

　第 4 段落第 2 文後半参照。aim は「目的，目標」の意味で，具体的な内容が to allow 以下に書かれている。

問4

(ア) 以下のポイントをおさえよう！

☑ who は関係代名詞で，先行詞は the man。

☑ dynamite の後の「コンマ(,)」は【**同格**】を表す。〈名詞 A，名詞 B〉で A と B が同格となる場合，「**A つまり B，A という B，A である B**」（それぞれ A と B を逆にしても可）などの訳が可能。

(イ) 以下のポイントをおさえよう！

☑ the Bank of Sweden が S，added が V，a prize in economics が O。

☑ to celebrate 以下は不定詞の副詞用法で【**目的**】を表す。

☑ celebrate は「〜を祝う，記念する」。

☑ the bank's 300th year of business は直訳すれば「その銀行の営業の 300 年目」。「同行の創業 300 周年」など自然な日本語にするとよい。

なお，Later をより具体的に言い換えたのが，コンマの後ろの in 1968 である。

第1段落　文の構造と語句のチェック

¹(Each year)(on December 10), <u>the world's attention</u> <u>turns</u> (to Sweden)
　　　　　　　　　　　　　　　　　　　　 S　　　　　　　　 V

(for the announcement 〔 of the Nobel Prize winners 〕). ²<u>The Nobel Prizes, six</u>
　　　　　　　　　　　　　　　　　　　　　　　　　　　　　　　　 S　　└同格─┘

<u>prizes</u> 〔 given to <u>groups</u> or <u>individuals</u> 〔 <u>who</u> really <u>stand out</u> (in their fields)〕〕,
　　　　　　　　　① 等接 ②　　　　　 関代　　　 V

<u>were founded</u> (by a <u>Swedish inventor, Alfred Nobel</u>).
　　 V　　　　　　　　　　　　　 └同格─┘

> **訳** ¹毎年12月10日，世界の注目はノーベル賞受賞者の発表のためスウェーデンに向けられる。²ノーベル賞は，各自の分野で本当に際立った団体または個人に与えられる6つの賞で，スウェーデンの発明家であるアルフレッド・ノーベルによって創立された。

Check! 第2文 The Nobel Prizes, six prizes given to groups or individuals who really stand out in their fields, were founded by a Swedish inventor, Alfred Nobel. の The Nobel Prizes と six prizes … fields，そして a Swedish inventor と Alfred Nobel が，それぞれ【同格】になっている。〈名詞 A，名詞 B〉で，A と B のいずれかを取り除いても文が成立する場合，A と B が同格〔言い換え〕となっている場合が多い。

語句

each year	熟	毎年	winner	名 受賞者
attention	名	注意，注目	individual	名 個人
turn to ~	熟	~に向く	stand out	熟 目立つ，注目を浴びる
announcement	名	発表	field	名 分野
prize	名	賞	found	動 創立する，設立する
			inventor	名 発明家

第2段落 文の構造と語句のチェック

¹Alfred Nobel was the man〔who invented dynamite, a powerful explosive〕.
 S   V   C 関代   V   O └─同格─┘

²(During his life), Nobel made a lot of money (from his invention), and he
            S   V   O   等接 S

decided〈 that he wanted to use his money (to help scientists, artists, and
 V   O 従接 S   V   O   V' ①   ②   等接

③
people〔who worked (to help others around the world)〕)〉. ³(When he died),
 関代 V   従接 S V

his will said〈 that the money would be placed (in a bank), and the interest
 S   V O 従接 S   V   等接   S
┌─ 関代 which 省略
〔the money earned〕would be given out (as five annual cash prizes)〉.
 S'   V'   V

> 訳 ¹アルフレッド・ノーベルは、ダイナマイトという強力な爆発物を発明した人物である。²生涯の間に、ノーベルは発明により多くの金を稼いだ。そして、彼は自分の金を、科学者や芸術家、そして世界中の他者を助けるために働いている人々を援助するために使いたいと心に決めた。³彼が死んだとき、彼の遺言には、その金は銀行に預け、その金で得た利子は毎年5つの賞金として分配するものとする、とあった。

Check! 第3文 ... and the interest the money earned would be given out as five annual cash prizes. の interest の後に、関係代名詞 which[that] が省略されている。

語句
invent	動 発明する	place	動 預ける
dynamite	名 ダイナマイト	interest	名 利子、利息
powerful	形 強力な	earn	動 稼ぐ、（利子が）つく
explosive	名 爆発物	give out ~	熟 ~を分配する
invention	名 発明	annual	形 毎年の
will	名 遺書、遺言	cash	名 現金
		▶ cash prize	名 賞金

27

第3段落　文の構造と語句のチェック

[1]The prizes 〔 set up by Nobel 〕 were first handed out (in 1901), and included
　　　S　　　　　　　　　　　　　　V①　　　　　　　　　　等接　　V②

①　　　　②　　　　　③　　　　　④　　　　　⑤
physics, medicine, chemistry, literature, and peace.　[2](Later), (in 1968) the
　　　　　　　　　O　　　　　　　　　等接

Bank of Sweden added a prize in economics (to celebrate the bank's 300th year
　　　S　　　　 V　　　O　　　　　　　　　　　V′　　　　　　O′

of business).

> **訳** [1]ノーベルによって創設された賞は 1901 年に初めて授与され，物理学賞，医学賞，化学賞，文学賞，平和賞から成っていた。[2]後に，1968 年に，スウェーデン国立銀行が同行の創業 300 周年を記念して経済学の分野での賞を加えた。

語句

set up ~	熟	~を創設する，設ける		literature	名	文学
hand out ~	熟	~を配る，~を手渡す		peace	名	平和
include	動	含む		later	副	後に
physics	名	物理学		add	動	加える
medicine	名	医学		economics	名	経済学
chemistry	名	化学		celebrate	動	祝う，記念する
				business	名	事業，営業

第4段落　文の構造と語句のチェック

　　　　　　　　　　　　　　　　　　　　　　　　　①　　　　　　②　　　　等接
[1]Each person 〔 who receives a Nobel Prize 〕 is given a cash prize, a medal, and
　　S　　　　　関代　 V　　　O　　　　　　　V　　　　　　　　O

③
a certificate.　[2]The prize money 〔 for each category 〕 is currently worth
　　　　　　　　　　　S　　　　　　　　　　　　　　　　V

about a million dollars, and the aim of the prize is 〈 to allow the winner to carry
　　　　C　　　　　　　等接　　　S　　　　　　　V C　V′　　　O′

①　　　　　②
on working or researching (without having to worry (about raising money))〉.
　C′　　等接

> **訳** ¹ノーベル賞の各受賞者は賞金とメダルと証明書を授与される。²各部門の賞金は現在のところ，およそ 100 万ドル相当となっており，この賞の目的は，受賞者が資金調達を心配する必要なく仕事や研究を続けられるようにすることである。

Check! 第 2 文の worth は前置詞（形容詞という考え方もある）で「～の価値があ
る，～に値する」。

> **例** This watch is worth 1,000 dollars.
> 「この時計は 1000 ドルの価値がある」

Check! 第 2 文の allow O to *do* は「O が～することを許可する」のほか，「O が～
することを可能にする」の意味もある。

　第 2 文の without having to worry … は，without *doing*「～せずに」と have
to *do*「～しなければならない」が組み合わさった表現。

語句

receive	動 受け取る	**worth**	前 ～の価値がある
medal	名 メダル，勲章	**aim**	名 目的，目標
certificate	名 証明書	**allow**	動 可能にする
category	名 部門，区分	carry on *doing*	熟 ～し続ける
currently	副 現在のところ	**raise**	動 （金を）集める，調達する

第 5 段落　文の構造と語句のチェック

¹The prizes <u>can be given</u> (to **either** individuals **or** groups). ²<u>Prize winners</u>
　S　　　　V　　　　　　　　　　　　　　　　　　　　　　　　　　　　　　　　　S

<u>include</u> <u>Albert Einstein</u> (physics, 1921), <u>Kenzaburo Oe</u> (literature, 1994),
　V　　　　　O①　　　　　　　　　　　　　　　　O②

<u>Kim Dae Jung</u> (peace, 2001), <u>the United Nations</u> (peace, 2001), **and**
　O③　　　　　　　　　　　　　　　O④　　　　　　　　　　　　　　　　等接

<u>Nelson Mandela</u> (peace, 1993).
　O⑤

29

¹ノーベル賞は個人または団体のいずれかに授与されうる。²受賞者には，アルバート・アインシュタイン(物理学賞，1921 年)や，大江健三郎(文学賞，1994 年)，金大中(平和賞，2001 年)，国際連合(平和賞，2001 年)，ネルソン・マンデラ(平和賞，1993 年)などがいる。

語句

either *A* or *B* 　熟　A か B のいずれか

第6段落 　文の構造と語句のチェック

¹The prize winner 〔 that has won (the most times)〕 is the International
　S　　　　　　　　　関代　V　　　(the most times)　　　V

Committee for the Red Cross. ²This organization has received three Nobel
　　　　　C　　　　　　　　　　　S　　　　　　　V

Peace Prizes (in 1917, 1944, and 1963), and the founder, Jean Henri Dunant,
　O　　　　　　　　　　　　　　　　　　　　　等接　　S　└─同格─┘

was awarded the first Nobel Peace Prize, (in 1901).
　V　　　　　O

訳 ¹最も受賞回数の多い受賞者は，赤十字国際委員会である。²この団体はノーベル平和賞を 3 回(1917 年，1944 年，1963 年)受賞し，創立者であるジャン・アンリ・デュナンは 1901 年に第 1 回ノーベル平和賞を授与された。

語句

committee	名 委員会	**founder**	名 創立者
organization	名 組織，団体	**award**	動 (賞を)与える，授与する

文法事項の整理 ②　挿入句

第 1 段落第 2 文の挿入句についてみてみよう。

The Nobel Prizes, six prizes given to groups or individuals who really stand out in their fields, were founded by ...

コンマ(,)で挟まれていて，その部分をとばして読んでも前後がつながるような場合，【挿入句】という。働きを整理しよう。

(1) 直前部分と同格(言い換え)

▶「つまり」「すなわち」「という」「である」などと訳す。

例　Tokyo, the capital of Japan, is an exciting city.
「日本の首都である東京は，わくわくする都市である」

(2) 主節にあたるものの挿入　▶最初か最後に訳す。

例　Your plan is, everybody will agree, not easy to carry out.
「みんな意見が一致するだろうが，君の計画は実行するのが容易ではない」
(= Everybody will agree (that) your plan is not easy to carry out.)

(3) 副詞(句・節)の挿入　▶語順どおりでも，最初に訳してもよい。

例　You should, if possible, go to the dentist.
「君は，可能なら歯医者に行くべきだ[可能なら，君は歯医者に行くべきだ]」
※ただし，論理関係を示す副詞が挿入されている場合，必ず最初に訳す。

例　He isn't a hardworking student. In the exams, however, he always gets a high score.
「彼は勤勉な学生ではない。しかし，試験ではいつも高得点を取る」

■第 1 段落第 2 文

The Nobel Prizes, six prizes given to groups or individuals who really stand out in their fields, were founded by ...　▶(1)の同格の用法。

■第 6 段落第 2 文

..., and the founder, Jean Henri Dunant, was awarded the first Nobel Peace Prize, in 1901.　▶(1)の同格の用法。

確認問題

1. 次の和訳と対応する英語の語句を，頭文字を参考にして書き，空欄を完成させよう。

（各1点×20）

#			
①	a	名	注意，注目
②	a	名	発表
③	p	名	賞
④	i	名	個人
⑤	s ___ o	熟	目立つ，注目を浴びる
⑥	f	動	創立する，設立する
⑦	w	名	遺書，遺言
⑧	i	名	利子，利息
⑨	p	名	物理学
⑩	m	名	医学
⑪	c	名	化学
⑫	l	名	文学
⑬	c	動	祝う，記念する
⑭	r	動	受け取る
⑮	c	名	証明書
⑯	a	名	目的，目標
⑰	r	動	(金を)集める，調達する
⑱	c	名	委員会
⑲	o	名	組織，団体
⑳	a	動	(賞を)与える，授与する

2. 次の[　]内の語句を並べ替えて，意味の通る英文を完成させよう。（各5点×2）

① When he died, his will said that the money would be placed in a bank, and the [be / money / the / would / interest / earned] given out as five

32

annual cash prizes.

② The prizes [individuals / given / either / be / or / to / can] groups.

3. 次の英文を和訳してみよう。(10 点)

The Nobel Prizes, six prizes given to groups or individuals who really stand out in their fields, were founded by a Swedish inventor, Alfred Nobel.

ディクテーションしてみよう！

今回学習した英文に出てきた語句・表現を，＿＿＿に書き取ろう。

05 10

05　Each year on December 10, the world's attention turns to Sweden for the announcement of the Nobel Prize winners. The Nobel Prizes, six prizes given to groups or individuals who really ❶＿＿＿＿＿＿＿＿ in their fields, ❷＿＿＿＿＿＿＿＿＿ by a Swedish inventor, Alfred Nobel.

06　Alfred Nobel was the man who invented dynamite, a powerful explosive. During his life, Nobel made a lot of money from his invention, and he decided that he wanted to use his money to help scientists, artists, and people who worked to help others around the world. When he died, ❸＿＿＿＿＿＿＿＿ that the money would be placed in a bank, and the interest the money earned would be ❹＿＿＿＿＿＿＿ as five annual cash prizes.

07　The prizes ❺＿＿＿＿＿ by Nobel were first handed out in ❻＿＿＿＿, and included physics, medicine, chemistry, literature, and peace. Later, in 1968 the Bank of Sweden added a ❼＿＿＿＿＿＿＿ ＿＿＿＿＿ to celebrate the bank's 300th year of business.

08　Each person who receives a Nobel Prize is given a cash prize, a medal, and a certificate. The prize money for each category is ❽＿＿＿＿ ＿＿＿＿＿＿＿＿ about a million dollars, and the aim of the prize is to allow the winner to carry on working or researching without having to worry about raising money.

09　The prizes can be given to either individuals or groups. Prize winners include Albert Einstein (physics, 1921), Kenzaburo Oe (literature, 1994), Kim Dae Jung (peace, 2001), the United Nations (peace, 2001), and Nelson Mandela (peace, 1993).

10　The prize winner that ❾＿＿＿＿＿＿＿ the most times is the International Committee for the Red Cross. This organization has received three Nobel Peace Prizes (in 1917, 1944, and 1963), and the founder, Jean Henri Dunant, ❿＿＿＿＿＿＿＿＿＿＿ the first Nobel Peace Prize, in 1901.

確認問題の答　　1.　① attention　② announcement　③ prize　④ individual
⑤ stand out　⑥ found　⑦ will　⑧ interest　⑨ physics　⑩ medicine
⑪ chemistry　⑫ literature　⑬ celebrate　⑭ receive　⑮ certificate
⑯ aim　⑰ raise　⑱ committee　⑲ organization　⑳ award

2.　① interest the money earned would be　（第2段落　第3文）
② can be given to either individuals or　（第5段落　第1文）

3.　ノーベル賞は，各自の分野で本当に際立った団体または個人に与えられる6つの賞で，スウェーデンの発明家であるアルフレッド・ノーベルによって創立された。　（第1段落　第2文）

ディクテーションしてみよう！の答　　❶ stand out　❷ were founded　❸ his will said
❹ given out　❺ set up　❻ 1901　❼ prize in economics　❽ currently worth
❾ has won　❿ was awarded

アドバイス　❸ will の名詞としての用法を知らないと聞き取れないだろう。

❼ prize の /z/ の音と後ろの i, in の /n/ の音と後ろの e がそれぞれつながり，「ジネ」のように聞こえる（⇒連結）。

❾ won の発音は one と同じ。「ウォン」などと読んでいては聞き取れないはずだ。

3 解答・解説

問題は別冊 p.08

解 答

問1	②	問2	③	問3	①	問4	②
問5	④	問6	④	問7	③, ④, ⑤		

解 説

問1

fast は「断食する」の意味の動詞。意味を知らなくても，文頭にある**【逆接】を表す However「しかし」**の働きや，第1段落第1文の stop eating が主題を提示している点に注目すれば，推測は可能。

問2

空所直前の前置詞 in と合わせて各選択肢の意味を検討すると，① in turn「順番に，同様に」，② in detail「詳細に」，③ in protest「抗議して」，④ in competition「競争して」となる。第2段落第2文で女性に投票権がなかったこと，空所を含む第2段落第3文では女性による断食の実行について書かれているので，③が正解。

問3

justice は「公平，公正」の意味で，**否定の接頭辞 in- が付いた injustice は「不公平，不公正」の意味**になる。また，this は前出の内容（多くは直前の文に含まれる）を指す。ここでは，第2段落第2文の内容（女性に投票権が認められていなかったこと）を指していると考えれば，injustice の語義と合う。

問4

接続詞 as は**【時】【理由】【様態】【比例】**などの意味を持つが，**【様態】「…するように，…するとおりに」**の意味の場合，本文のように as 以下で倒置が起こり，**〈as＋be[do / have など]＋S〉の語順になることがある**。**【様態】の as は主節と従属節の内容が共通していることを示す。**

> **例** John is very clever, **as** *is* his brother.
> 「ジョンは，彼の兄がそうであるように，非常に賢い」

ここでの do の内容は，「ヒンドゥー教徒」との共通点を挙げている文脈なの

35

で，fast on special occasions を指すと考えるべき。よって②が正解。

問5

各選択肢の意味は，①「食べ物」，②「よく売れるもの，販売者」，③「場所」，④「薬」。直後の2文で，断食をすることで風邪や発熱がなくなったとあるので，④が適切。

問6

本文で一貫して論じられているのは「断食の理由」である。第1段落は主題を提示し，第2段落は政治的理由による断食，第3段落は宗教的理由による断食，第4段落は健康上の理由による断食について述べられている。したがって，④「食べ物なしで過ごす理由」が正解。

問7

① 「私たちは余分なカロリーを身体にため込まないためには身体的に活発でなくてはならない」
▶ そのような記述はない。

② 「モーハンダース・ガンジーは政治的な手段として断食をしたのではない」
▶ 第2段落第6文と不一致。

③ **「セザール・チャベスは政治的理由により断食をした」**
▶ 第2段落第9〜12文と一致。なお，第2段落第1文に for political reasons とあるので，この段落の3つの具体例はいずれも政治的理由と考えてよい。

④ **「マーク・トウェインは断食が風邪を治す有効な方法だと思っていた」**
▶ 第4段落第3〜5文と一致。

⑤ **「アプトン・シンクレアはかつて，たくさん食べて，胃の不調に苦しんだ」**
▶ 第4段落第6文と一致。

⑥ 「今日では人々はもう断食をしない」
▶ 第1段落第3文，第2段落第1文，第4段落第2文，最終段落第2文など，「人々が断食をする」との内容の英文がいずれも現在形で書かれているので，現在でも断食が行われていることがわかる。

⑦ 「医学的な問題に苦しんでいる患者を除けば，断食は危険である」
▶ 最終段落第1文に断食の危険性についての記述があるが，例外については特に書かれていない。

それでは次に，段落ごとに詳しくみていこう。

第1段落　文の構造と語句のチェック

¹Why would someone decide to stop eating? ²We know 〈 that the body needs
　　(V)　　S　　　　V　　　　O　　　　　S　　V　　O従接　　S　　　　V

food (in order to function well)〉. ³However, many people fast (at some time)
　O　　　　　　　　　　　　　　　　　　　　　　　　　S　　　　V

(during their lives). ⁴Why is this?
　　　　　　　　　　　　　　　　V　S

> 訳 ¹なぜ人は食べるのをやめようと決意するのだろうか。²身体は正しく機能するために食べ物を必要としていることを私たちは知っている。³しかし，多くの人々は人生の何らかの時に断食を行う。⁴これはなぜだろうか。

語句

in order to *do*	熟 〜するために	**however**	副 しかし
function	動 機能する	**fast**	動 断食する／名 断食

第2段落　文の構造と語句のチェック

¹Some people fast (for political reasons). ²(In the early 20th century),
　S　　　　V

women 〔 in England and the United States 〕 weren't allowed to vote. ³(In
　S　　　　①　　等接　　　②　　　　　　　　　　V

protest), many women went on fasts. ⁴They hoped 〈 that fasting would bring
　　　　　S　　　　　V　　　　　S　　V　　O従接　　S　　　　V

attention (to this injustice)〉. ⁵Mohandas Gandhi, the famous Indian leader,
　O　　　　　　　　　　　　　　　　　S　　　同格

fasted (17 times) (during his life). ⁶(For Gandhi), <u>fasting</u> <u>was</u> <u>a powerful</u>
<u>　V　</u>　　　　　　　　　　　　　　　　　　　　　　S　　V

<u>political tool</u>. ⁷(In 1943), <u>he</u> <u>fasted</u> (<u>to bring</u> <u>attention</u> (to his country's need
　　C　　　　　　　　　　　S　V　　　V'　　O'

[for independence])). ⁸(For 21 days), <u>he</u> <u>went without</u> <u>food</u>. ⁹<u>Another famous</u>
　　　　　　　　　　　　　　　　　　S　　　V　　　O　　　　　S

<u>faster</u> <u>was</u> <u>Cesar Chavez</u>. ¹⁰(In the 1960s), <u>he</u> <u>fasted</u> (for three weeks).
　V　　　　　　C　　　　　　　　　　　　　S　　V

¹¹<u>Why?</u> ¹²<u>His goal</u> <u>was</u> ⟨ <u>to bring</u> <u>attention</u> (to the terrible working conditions
　　　　　　S　　　V　C　　V'　　O'

[of farm workers in the United States])⟩.

訳 ¹政治的な理由で断食をする人々もいる。²20世紀初頭，イギリスやアメリカの女性たち
は投票が許されていなかった。³それに抗議して，多くの女性たちが断食を行った。⁴彼女た
ちは断食がこのような不公平への注意を喚起することを望んでいた。⁵インドの有名な指導
者であるモーハンダース・ガンジーは，生涯に17回の断食を行った。⁶ガンジーにとって
は，断食は強力な政治的手段だったのだ。⁷1943年に彼は，母国の独立の必要性に注意を
喚起するために断食をした。⁸21日間，彼は食料なしで過ごしたのだ。⁹もう1人，断食を
した有名人にセザール・チャベスがいる。¹⁰1960年代に彼は3週間の断食をした。¹¹なぜか。
¹²彼の目的はアメリカの農場労働者たちのひどい労働条件に注意を喚起することであった。

語句

political	形	政治的な
century	名	世紀
allow	動	許可する
vote	動	投票する
protest	名	抗議
▶**in protest**	熟	抗議して
go on a fast	熟	断食する
attention	名	注意，注目
▶**bring attention to ~**		
	熟	～への注意を喚起する

injustice	名	不公平，不公正
famous	形	有名な
leader	名	指導者
powerful	形	強力な
tool	名	道具，手段
independence	名	独立
go without ~	熟	～なしで済ます
faster	名	断食する人
goal	名	目標，目的
terrible	形	ひどい，ひどく悪い
condition	名	条件，状況

第3段落 文の構造と語句のチェック

[1]Fasting <u>is</u> also <u>a spiritual practice</u> (in many religions). [2](Every year)
　S　　V　　　　　C

(during the month of Ramadan), **which** <u>is</u> <u>a religious holiday</u>, <u>Muslims</u> <u>fast</u>
　　　　　　　　　　　　　　　　　関代　V　　　　C　　　　　S　　　V

(**from** sunrise **to** sunset). [3]<u>Many Hindus</u> <u>fast</u> (on special occasions), (**as** <u>do</u>
　　　　　　　　　　　　　　　　S　　　　V　　　　　　　　　　　　　従接　V

<u>some Christians</u> **and** <u>Buddhists</u>).
　①　　　　　　等接②
　　　　S

> **訳** [1]断食はまた，多くの宗教における精神修行でもある。[2]毎年，宗教上の祭日であるラマ
> ダン月の間，イスラム教徒は日の出から日没まで断食をする。[3]多くのヒンドゥー教徒は，
> 一部のキリスト教徒や仏教徒と同様，特別な時に断食をする。

Check! 第3文 Many Hindus fast on special occasions, as do some Christians and Buddhists. の do は，前出の fast on special occasions の代用。as は【様態】の接続詞で，as の後では倒置が起こることがある。ここでは，do(=V) some Christians and Buddhists(=S)と倒置が起こっている。

語句

spiritual	形 精神的な		**religious**	形 宗教的な
practice	名 訓練，練習		sunrise	名 日の出
religion	名 宗教		sunset	名 日没
			occasion	名 時，場合

第4段落 文の構造と語句のチェック

[1](Of course), <u>not everyone</u> <u>fasts</u> (for <u>political</u> **or** <u>religious</u> reasons).
　　　　　　　　　　S　　　　　V　　　　　①　　等接　　②

[2]<u>Some people</u> occasionally <u>fast</u> (just **because** <u>it</u> <u>makes</u> <u>them</u> <u>feel better</u>). [3]<u>The</u>
　　S　　　　　　　　　　V　　　　従接　S　　V　　O　　　C

　　　　　　　　　　　　　　　　　　　　┌─ 従接 that 省略
<u>American writer</u> <u>Mark Twain</u> <u>thought</u> (<u>fasting</u> <u>was</u> <u>the best medicine</u> [for
　S　　　└─同格─┘　　V　　　O　　　S　　　V　　　　C

39

common illnesses)⟩. ⁴(Whenever he had a cold or a fever), he stopped eating
　　　　　　　　　　　 従接　　S　 V　①　 ②　 等接　　　　 S　　 V　　　O

completely. ⁵He said ⟨ that this always made his cold or fever go away ⟩.
　　　　　　　　 S　 V　 O 従接　S　　　　　 V　　①　 ②　等接　 C

⁶Another American writer, Upton Sinclair, discovered fasting (after years of
　　　　　　　　　　　　 S　└─同格─┘　　　　　 V　　　 O

overeating, stomach problems, and headaches). ⁷His first fast lasted (for 12
　　①　　　　　 ②　　　 等接　　③　　　　　　　S　　　　　 V

days). ⁸(During this time), his headaches and stomachaches went away.
　　　　　　　　　　　　　　　　　①　　　 等接 ②　　 V

⁹Sinclair said ⟨ that fasting also made him more alert and energetic ⟩.
　　 S　　　 V　 O 従接　S　　　　 V　 O　　 C　 等接

> **訳** ¹もちろん，誰もが政治的あるいは宗教的な理由で断食をするわけではない。²単に気分を良くしてくれるからという理由で時々断食をする人もいる。³アメリカ人作家であるマーク・トウェインは，断食がよくある病気に対する最良の薬であると考えた。⁴彼は風邪を引いたり発熱したりするたびに，完全に食べることをやめた。⁵いつもこれによって風邪や発熱が治るのだと彼は言った。⁶また別のアメリカ人作家，アプトン・シンクレアは，長年にわたる過食，胃の不調，そして頭痛の末に断食を知った。⁷彼の初めての断食は 12 日間続いた。⁸この間に彼の頭痛や胃痛は治った。⁹シンクレアは，断食によってさらに頭の回転が速くなり精力的にもなると言った。

Check! 第 1 文 Of course, not everyone fasts for political or religious reasons. の not everyone は，「誰もが～というわけではない」の意味で【部分否定】を表す。

Check! 第 2 文 Some people occasionally fast just because it makes them feel better. の just because ... は「単に…というだけの理由で」の意味。simply because ... や merely because ... も同様の意味。

語句

of course	熟	もちろん
occasionally	副	時々，たまに
writer	名	作家
medicine	名	薬
common	形	一般的な，普通の
illness	名	病気
whenever	接	～するときはいつでも，～するたびに
cold	名	風邪
fever	名	熱，発熱

completely	副	完全に
go away	熟	消える，（病気が）治る
discover	動	発見する，気づく
overeating	名	過食
stomach	名	胃
headache	名	頭痛
last	動	続く，持続する
stomachache	名	胃痛
alert	形	機敏な，頭の回転が速い
energetic	形	精力的な

第5段落　文の構造と語句のチェック

¹〈 Choosing to go without food 〉 <u>can be</u> <u>very dangerous</u>.　²However, <u>that</u>
　S　　　　　　　　　　　　　　　　　　 V　　　　　C　　　　　　　　　　　　　　S

<u>doesn't</u> <u>stop</u> <u>people</u> (<u>from</u> fasting (for political, religious, or health reasons)).
　V　　　　 O　　　　　①　　　　　　　②　　　　　 等接　　③

訳 ¹食べ物なしで過ごすという選択は非常に危険な場合もある。²しかし，それでも人々は政治的，宗教的，あるいは健康上の理由から断食をすることをやめない。

語句

choose	動	選択する
stop O from *doing*	熟	O が～するのをやめさせる，O に～させない

文法事項の整理 ③　部分否定

第4段落第1文の not everyone についてみてみよう。

Of course, **not everyone** fasts for political or religious reasons.

「全部が～というわけではない，いつも～というわけではない」といった「例外を認める否定」を【部分否定】という。

■部分否定の形

(1) 副詞による部分否定

not ＋ always	「いつも [必ずしも] 〜というわけではない」
not ＋ necessarily	「必ずしも〜というわけではない」
not ＋ everywhere	「どこでも〜というわけではない」
not ＋ quite altogether completely entirely wholly	「まったく [完全に] 〜というわけではない」
not ＋ very much so too	「あまり [それほど / たいして] 〜というわけではない」

(2) 代名詞・形容詞による部分否定と全体否定

	2者	3者以上
部分否定	・not＋both (形 代) 「両方〜というわけではない」	・not＋all (形 代) ・not＋every (形) 　「すべて〜というわけではない」
全体否定	・not＋either (形 代) 　*either＋not は× ・neither (形 代) 「どちらも〜ない」	・not＋any (形 代) 　*any＋not は× ・no (形) ・none (代) 「まったく [1つも] 〜ない」

※ 形：形容詞の働きをし，直後に名詞がつく。
　 代：代名詞の働きをし，単独でSやOになる。

■第4段落第1文

Of course, **not everyone** fasts for political or religious reasons.

▶ 〈not＋every-〉なので，3者以上についての部分否定。

確認問題

1. 次の和訳と対応する英語の語句を，頭文字を参考にして書き，空欄を完成させよう。

（各1点×20）

①	f	動	機能する
②	p	形	政治的な
③	a	動	許可する
④	v	動	投票する
⑤	p	名	抗議
⑥	i	名	不公平，不公正
⑦	i	名	独立
⑧	g	名	目標，目的
⑨	c	名	条件，状況
⑩	s	形	精神的な
⑪	r	名	宗教
⑫	o	副	時々，たまに
⑬	m	名	薬
⑭	c	形	一般的な，普通の
⑮	f	名	熱，発熱
⑯	c	副	完全に
⑰	d	動	発見する，気づく
⑱	s	名	胃
⑲	e	形	精力的な
⑳	c	動	選択する

2. 次の[　]内の語句を並べ替えて，意味の通る英文を完成させよう。（各5点×2）

① They hoped that [injustice / attention / this / would / to / fasting / bring].

② Sinclair said that [more / made / also / fasting / alert / him] and energetic.

Of course, not everyone fasts for political or religious reasons.

ディクテーションしてみよう！

今回学習した英文に出てきた語句・表現を，＿＿＿＿に書き取ろう。

12・16

12 Why would someone decide to stop eating? We know that the body needs food ❶＿＿＿＿＿＿＿＿＿＿ function well. However, many people fast at some time during their lives. Why is this?

13 Some people fast for political reasons. In the early 20th century, women in England and the United States weren't ❷＿＿＿＿＿＿＿＿＿＿＿＿＿ ＿＿＿＿＿. In protest, many women went on fasts. They hoped that fasting would bring attention to this injustice. Mohandas Gandhi, the famous Indian leader, fasted ❸＿＿＿＿＿＿＿＿＿＿＿＿＿＿＿ during his life. For Gandhi, fasting was a powerful political tool. In 1943, he fasted to bring attention to his country's need for independence. For 21 days, he ❹＿＿＿＿＿＿＿＿＿＿ food. Another famous faster was Cesar Chavez. In the 1960s, he fasted for three weeks. Why? His goal was to bring attention to the terrible ❺＿＿＿＿＿＿＿＿＿＿＿＿＿ of farm workers in the United States.

14 Fasting is also a spiritual practice in many ❻＿＿＿＿＿＿. Every year during the month of Ramadan, which is a religious holiday, Muslims fast from sunrise to sunset. Many Hindus fast on special occasions, ❼＿＿＿＿ some Christians and Buddhists.

15 Of course, not everyone fasts for political or religious reasons. Some people occasionally fast just because it makes them ❽＿＿＿＿＿＿＿＿＿. The American writer Mark Twain thought fasting was the best medicine for common illnesses. Whenever he had a cold or a fever, he stopped eating completely. He said that this always made his cold or fever go away. Another American writer, Upton Sinclair, discovered fasting after years of overeating, stomach problems, and headaches. His ❾_____ lasted for 12 days. During this time, his headaches and stomachaches ❿_____. Sinclair said that fasting also made him more alert and energetic.

16　Choosing to go without food can be very dangerous. However, that doesn't stop people from fasting for political, religious, or health reasons.

確認問題の答　**1.** ① function　② political　③ allow　④ vote　⑤ protest
　　　　　　　　⑥ injustice　⑦ independence　⑧ goal　⑨ condition　⑩ spiritual
　　　　　　　　⑪ religion　⑫ occasionally　⑬ medicine　⑭ common　⑮ fever
　　　　　　　　⑯ completely　⑰ discover　⑱ stomach　⑲ energetic　⑳ choose
　2. ① fasting would bring attention to this injustice　（第 2 段落　第 4 文）
　　　② fasting also made him more alert　（第 4 段落　最終文）
　3. もちろん，誰もが政治的あるいは宗教的な理由で断食をするわけではない。　（第 4 段落　第 1 文）

ディクテーションしてみよう！の答　❶ in order to　❷ allowed to vote　❸ 17[seventeen] times
　　❹ went without　❺ working conditions　❻ religions　❼ as do　❽ feel better
　　❾ first fast　❿ went away

アドバイス　❷単語の正しい発音を知っておく必要がある。allow を arrow と混同して「アロー」などと発音しているようで
　　は聞き取れない。
　　❸ 17(seventeen) か 70(seventy) か，聞き取りのポイントはアクセントの位置。seventeen は第 3 音節，
　　seventy は第 1 音節にアクセントが置かれる。
　　❽ /t/ や /d/ の音が母音に挟まれると，「ら行」のような音になる（⇒フラッピング）。better は「ベター」とい
　　うより「ベラ」のように聞こえる。

4 解答・解説

解答

問1	③	問2	③	問3	②	問4	④	問5	③
問6	④	問7	②	問8	④	問9	①	問10	③

解説

問1 「多くの人々が知らないことは何か」

① 「小さな成功は失敗と異なることが多い」

② 「失敗と成功は異なることが多い」

③ **「成功と失敗の間には小さな違いがあることが多い」**

④ 「失敗とは小さな成功であることが多い」

▶ 第1段落第1文参照。

問2 「金メダルを獲得する人物は＿＿＿＿＿人であることが多い」

① 「10倍速い」

② 「2倍速い」

③ **「少しだけ速い」**

④ 「決してあきらめない」

▶ 第3段落第4, 5文参照。

問3 「『小さな違いが大きな違いを作り出すかもしれない』は＿＿＿＿＿ということを意味する」

① 「成功はちょっとした運によることが多い」

② **「成功は小さな事柄によることが多い」**

③ 「決してあきらめてはならない」

④ 「人生はしばしば真実だ」

▶ 設問文中の引用部分は第1段落第4文と最終段落第6文にある。これらの前後の内容から考える。本文では「運」については言及されていないことに注意。

問4 「勝者と敗者の違いは＿＿＿＿＿ことが多い」

① 「かなり大きい」

② 「大きい」

③「2倍優れている」

④「たいしたことはない」

▶ 第1段落第3文，第3段落第3文参照。① quite a bit は「相当な，かなりの」（≒quite a little）の意味である点に注意。

問5　「本文によれば，_____はたいていの場合，成功につながる」

①「わずかな時だけ，大部分が優れていること」

②「ほとんどの時に，はるかに優れていること」

③「1，2パーセントを反復すること」

④「将来において完璧となること」

▶ 第4段落第1文参照。

問6　「本文によれば，もし_____ならば私たちはもっと成功できる」

①「私たちが天才である」

②「私たちが10倍優れている」

③「私たちが完璧である」

④「私たちが少しだけ優れている」

▶ 第4段落全体，および最終段落第4文参照。

問7　「英雄は_____」

①「とてつもない力を持っている」

②「たいてい少しだけ優れているので，成功する」

③「他者とは大きく異なる」

④「平均よりもさほど美しくない」

▶ 最終段落第1～3文参照。

問8　「第1段落の最後の部分で，"the small difference is regular and repeated" という表現は_____を意味している」

①「何度も繰り返し練習すること」

②「小さな違いとはわずか1，2パーセントでしかないことが多いこと」

③「小さな違い」

④「一連の小さな違い」

▶ 引用部分は「小さな違いが定期的で反復される」で，a series of ～ は「一連の～，ひと続きの～」という意味。この後の第2段落の具体例も参考になる。

問9　「本文の最後の "result" という語は＿＿＿＿＿のことを言っている」

① 「あなたの成功」

② 「あなたの努力」

③ 「より熱心に努力すること」

④ 「ちょっとした失敗」

▶ 最終段落後半は小さな努力の積み重ねが成功につながるという内容。したがって「結果」とは「成功」のことである。

問10　「本文に最も適切なタイトルはどれか」

① 「習うより慣れろ」

② 「小さな成功」

③ **「成功する方法」**

④ 「違いを生じさせない方法」

▶ 本文では成功と失敗の差はわずかであることを，具体例を挙げて示している。そして最終段落であともう少しの努力をすることを勧め，そのことが成功につながるのだとしている。よって③が正解。①は Practice makes perfect.「練習が完璧を作り上げる」→「習うより慣れろ」という意味のことわざ。

▼

それでは次に，段落ごとに詳しくみていこう。

17

第1段落　文の構造と語句のチェック

¹Many people don't know 〈 that the difference 〔 between success and failure 〕
　　S　　　　　V　　　　O 従接　　　　　　　　　　　S

is often very small 〉. ²One does not need to be twice as good, (let alone perfect),
V　　　　C　　　　　　　　S　　　　　　V　　　　　　C

(in order to succeed (in most things)). ³(In fact), often only a tiny difference
　　　　　　　　　　　　　　　　　　　　　　　　　　　　　　　　S

48

$$\underset{\text{V}}{\text{separates}} \underset{\text{O}}{\underset{①}{\text{winners}} \overset{\text{等接②}}{\text{and}} \text{losers.}} \quad {}^{4}\underset{\text{S}}{\text{A small difference}} \underset{\text{V}}{\text{may make}} \underset{\text{O}}{\text{a big difference.}}$$

$$\underset{\text{S}}{{}^{5}\text{This}} \underset{\text{V}}{\text{is}} \underset{\text{C}}{\text{true}} (\text{ in many areas of life }), (\text{ especially} \underset{\text{従接}}{\text{if}} \underset{\text{S}}{\text{the small difference}} \underset{\text{V}}{\text{is}}$$

$$\underset{\text{C}}{\underset{①}{\text{regular}} \overset{\text{等接②}}{\text{and}} \text{repeated}}).$$

> **訳** ¹多くの人々は，成功と失敗の違いがごく小さいものである場合が多いということを知らない。²ほとんどの物事において成功するためには，（他者より）2倍も優れている必要はなく，まして完璧である必要はないのだ。³実際は，ほんのちっぽけな差が勝者と敗者を分ける場合が多い。⁴小さな違いが大きな違いを作り出すかもしれないのだ。⁵このことは人生の多くの面において，特に小さな違いが定期的で反復される場合に当てはまる。

Check! 第2文 One does not need to be twice as good, let alone perfect, in order to succeed in most things. の主語 One は「一般の人」を表しており，通常は訳さない。

語句

difference	名	違い	tiny	形	とても小さい，ごくわずかの
success	名	成功	separate	動	分ける，（勝敗を）決める
failure	名	失敗	winner	名	勝者
let alone ~	熟	まして~はなおさら	loser	名	敗者
in order to do	熟	~するために	area	名	領域，分野
succeed	動	成功する	especially	副	特に
in fact	熟	実際に	regular	形	定期的な，いつもの
			repeat	動	反復する

第2段落　文の構造と語句のチェック

$${}^{1}(\text{ For example }), \underset{\text{V}}{\text{consider}} \underset{\text{O}}{\text{two clocks,}} [\text{ running at a speed } [\text{ differing only by}$$

$$\text{one second per hour }]]. \quad {}^{2}\underset{\text{S}}{\text{Only one second per hour}} \underset{\text{V}}{\text{doesn't seem}} \underset{\text{C}}{\text{like much,}} \underset{\text{等接}}{\text{but}}$$

it is almost a half minute per day, or almost three minutes a week, or
S V　　　　　　C①　　　　　　　　　　等接　　　　　　C②　　　　　　　　　等接

about twelve minutes a month, and almost two and a half hours a year. ³Well,
　　　　　C③　　　　　　　　等接　　　　C④

there's actually quite a difference (between those two clocks).
　　V　　　　　　　S

訳 ¹たとえば，1 時間につき 1 秒だけ異なるスピードで進む 2 つの時計を考えてみよう。
²1 時間につきたった 1 秒はたいしたことがないように思われるが，1 日あたりほぼ 30 秒
であり，1 週間あたりほぼ 3 分であり，1 カ月あたりほぼ 12 分であり，1 年あたりだと
ほぼ 2 時間半である。³そう，これらの 2 つの時計の間には実際にはかなりの違いが存在
するのだ。

語 句

for example	熟	たとえば
consider	動	考える，検討する
differ	動	異なる
second	名	秒

per	前	～につき，～ごとに
almost	副	ほぼ，ほとんど
actually	副	実際は
quite	副	かなり
▶ quite a ～	熟	かなりの～

第 3 段落　文の構造と語句のチェック

¹Sports is another good example. ²One doesn't have to be much better (than
S　　V　　　　　C　　　　　　　S　　　　　　　V　　　　C

others) (to win). ³The difference 〔 between winning and losing 〕 is often
　　　　　　　　　　　The difference
　　　　　　　　　　　　S　　　　　　　　　　　　　　　　　　　V

very small. ⁴(At the Olympics), the difference 〔 between winning and losing 〕
　　C　　　　　　　　　　　　　　　　the difference
　　　　　　　　　　　　　　　　　　　S

is often just 0.1 second or just a centimeter or two. ⁵Such a small difference
V　　　　　C①　　　　等接　　　　C②　　　　　　　　　　S

can determine 〈 who gets a gold medal 〉.
　　V　　　　　O 疑　V　　　O

50

訳 ¹スポーツはもう1つの好例だ。²勝つためには他者よりもずっと優れている必要はない。³勝つか負けるかの違いは非常に些細なものであることが多い。⁴オリンピックでは，勝敗の違いはわずか0.1秒あるいは1，2センチであることがよくある。⁵そのようなちょっとした差が，誰が金メダルを獲得するかを決定することがあり得るのだ。

Check! 第5文 Such a small difference can determine who gets a gold medal. の who は，関係代名詞ではなく疑問詞。「誰が～か」の意味で，名詞節を導く。ここでは who の導く節が determine の目的語になっている。

語句

another	形 他の，もう1つの		centimeter	名 センチメートル
example	名 例		**determine**	動 決定する，左右する
			medal	名 メダル

第4段落 文の構造と語句のチェック

¹A small difference, often just a percent or two, (if repeated over and over),
　 S 　　　└─同格─┘ 　　　　　　　従接　 └── it is 省略

will almost always lead to success 〔 in the future 〕. ²One does not need to be
　　　　　　　　V　　 O 　　　　　　　　　　　S　　 V①

a genius, does not need to be ten times better, or even twice as good, (let alone
　 C 　　　　 V② 　　　　　　　 ① 　　　等接 ② 　　　　　C

perfect). ³Just a small difference is usually enough (to succeed).
　　　　　　　　 S 　　　　　 V 　　 C

訳 ¹ちょっとした違い，しばしばたった1，2パーセントの違いが何度も反復されると，ほぼ確実に将来における成功につながるのだ。²天才である必要はなく，10倍も優れている必要はなく，2倍優れている必要さえなく，まして完璧である必要はない。³ほんのわずかの違いが，たいていの場合，成功するには十分なのだ。

percent	名 パーセント	future	名 未来，将来
over and over	熟 何度も繰り返し	genius	名 天才
lead to 〜	熟 〜につながる，〜を引き起こす		

第5段落 文の構造と語句のチェック

¹Our heroes seem to have superpowers, but actually they are just normal
　S　　　　V　　　　　O　　　　　等接　　　　　S　　V

people. ²They are not really that much different (from us). ³They are just a
　C　　　S　　V　　　　　　　　C　　　　　　　　　　　　S　　V

tiny bit faster, or smarter, or more beautiful (than average). ⁴(If one wants to
　　C①　　等接　C②　等接　　C③　　　　　　　　　　　　従接 S　　V

be successful), just remember 〈 that the difference 〔 between success and
　C　　　　　V　　　O 従接　　　S

failure 〕is often very small 〉. ⁵So why don't you try (just a little harder), (a
　　　　V　　　　C　　　　等接　（V）　S　V

little more often)? ⁶A small difference may make a big difference. ⁷You may be
　　　　　　　　　　　S　　　　　V　　　O　　　　　　　S　　V

surprised (by the result).
　C

> 訳 ¹私たちの英雄はとてつもない力を持っているように思われるが，実際には単なる普通
> の人々なのだ。²彼らは本当は私たちと大して変わらないのである。³ただ，平均よりもち
> ょっとだけ速かったり，頭が良かったり，美しかったりするだけなのだ。⁴もし成功したい
> のであれば，成功と失敗の違いは多くの場合，とてもわずかだということをとにかく忘れ
> ないことだ。⁵だから，もう少しだけ一生懸命に，もう少しだけ頻繁に，努力してみてはど
> うだろうか。⁶わずかな違いが大きな違いを生じるかもしれない。⁷その結果に驚かされる
> かもしれない。

語 句

hero	名 英雄	smart	形 利口な，頭の良い
superpower	名 非常に大きな力	average	名 平均
normal	形 普通の，標準の	successful	形 成功して
bit	名 ちょっと，少し	result	名 結果

文法事項の整理 ④ 副詞節中の〈S＋be〉の省略

第4段落第1文の if repeated over and over についてみてみよう。

A small difference, often just a percent or two, **if repeated over and over**, will almost always lead to success in the future.

　【時】【条件】【譲歩】の副詞節中の〈S＋be 動詞〉は，S が文全体の S と同じなら省略することができる。

＊**【時】**を表す副詞節：when ..., while ...,

＊**【条件】**を表す副詞節：if ..., unless ...,

＊**【譲歩】**を表す副詞節：though ..., although ...,

■副詞節中の〈S＋be 動詞〉の省略

例　She fell asleep while she was watching television. 【時】の副詞節
　　「彼女はテレビを見ている間に眠ってしまった」

例　This machine will be of great use if it is properly used.【条件】の副詞節
　　「この機械は適切に使えば非常に役立つ」

例　I didn't drink water though I was thirsty. 【譲歩】の副詞節
　　「私はのどが渇いていたが，水を飲まなかった」

　副詞節中の S が文全体の S と同じでなくても，文脈上明らかな場合は省略されることがある。

例　I will finish this work by tomorrow if it is possible.
　　「可能ならば明日までにこの仕事を終えるつもりだ」

■第4段落第1文

A small difference, often just a percent or two, <u>if repeated</u> over and over, will almost always lead to success in the future.

▶下線部は，if it is repeated の it is が省略されている（**【条件】**の副詞節）。

確認問題

1. 次の和訳と対応する英語の語句を，頭文字を参考にして書き，空欄を完成させよう。

（各1点×20）

①	d	名	違い
②	s	名	成功
③	f	名	失敗
④	l　　　a　　～	熟	まして～はなおさら
⑤	t	形	とても小さい，ごくわずかの
⑥	a	名	領域，分野
⑦	e	副	特に
⑧	r	形	定期的な，いつもの
⑨	c	動	考える，検討する
⑩	d	動	異なる
⑪	p	前	～につき，～ごとに
⑫	a	副	実際は
⑬	e	名	例
⑭	d	動	決定する，左右する
⑮	o　　　a　　　o	熟	何度も繰り返し
⑯	g	名	天才
⑰	n	形	普通の，標準の
⑱	s	形	利口な，頭の良い
⑲	a	名	平均
⑳	r	名	結果

2. 次の[　]内の語句を並べ替えて，意味の通る英文を完成させよう。（各5点×2）

① Many people don't know that [between / difference / success / and / the] failure is often very small.

54

② One [to / much / than / have / doesn't / better / be] others to win.

3. 次の英文を和訳してみよう。(10 点)

A small difference, often just a percent or two, if repeated over and over, will almost always lead to success in the future.

ディクテーションしてみよう！

今回学習した英文に出てきた語句・表現を，＿＿＿に書き取ろう。

18　Many people don't know that the difference between success ❶＿＿
＿＿＿＿＿＿＿＿＿ is often very small.　One does not need to be twice as good, ❷＿＿＿＿＿＿＿＿ perfect, in order to succeed in most things.　In fact, often only a tiny difference separates winners and losers.　A small difference may make a big difference.　This is true in many areas of life, especially if the small difference is regular and repeated.

19　For example, consider two clocks, running ❸＿＿＿＿＿＿＿＿ differing only by one second per hour.　Only one second per hour doesn't seem like much, but it is almost a half minute per day, or almost three minutes a week, or about twelve minutes a month, and almost ❹＿＿＿＿＿＿
＿＿＿＿＿＿＿＿＿＿＿ a year.　Well, there's actually quite a difference between those two clocks.

20　Sports is another good example.　One doesn't have to be much better than others to win.　The difference between winning and losing is often very small.　At the Olympics, the difference between winning and losing is often just 0.1 second or just a centimeter or two.　Such a small difference ❺＿＿＿
＿＿＿＿＿＿＿＿＿ who gets a gold medal.

21　A small difference, often just a percent or two, ❻＿＿＿＿＿＿＿＿
＿＿＿＿ over and over, will almost always lead to success in the future. One does not need to be a genius, does not need to be ten times better, or even twice as good, let alone perfect.　Just a small difference is usually

enough to succeed.

22 Our heroes seem to have superpowers, but actually they are just normal people. They are not really ❼＿＿＿＿＿＿＿＿＿＿＿＿＿＿

＿＿＿＿＿ from us. They are just a tiny bit faster, or smarter, or more beautiful than average. If one wants to be successful, just remember that the difference between success and failure is often very small. So ❽＿＿＿

＿＿＿＿＿＿＿＿＿＿＿＿＿＿＿ just a little harder, a little more often? A small difference may make a big difference. You may be surprised by the result.

解答

問	（ア） ③	（イ） ①	（ウ） ②	（エ） ③	（オ） ④

解説

問

（ア）「ドリス・ヴァン・カッペルホフは_____」

① 「卒業式に向かう途中，自動車事故で負傷した」

② 「将来はハリウッド映画の監督をしたいと思っていた」

③ **「ハリウッド映画に出るダンサーになることをあきらめた」**

④ 「数年間入院していた」

▶ ③が第1段落第2文と一致。①に関しては，第1段落第1文に「卒業パーティーの日の夜に」とあるが，「卒業式に行く途中で」とは書かれていない。②は監督をしたかったのではなく，映画のダンサーになりたかったと第1段落第2文に書かれているので不適。④は第1段落第3文と不一致。

（イ）「ドリスは_____によって歌の技術を向上させた」

① **「ラジオの女性歌手たちと一緒に歌うこと」**

② 「ハリウッド映画の中で役を演じること」

③ 「雇われてプロのバンドで歌うこと」

④ 「本当の天職を見つけること」

▶ 第1段落第3, 4文参照。選択肢②，③，④もそれぞれ近い記述はあるのだが，これらは歌の技術を向上させた手段ではなく，むしろその結果である。

（ウ）「筆者は私たちが_____と信じている」

① 「他人の行動のしかたをコントロールしようとしている」

② **「人生で何が起こるかを完全に知ることは決してできない」**

③ 「物事が自分の希望に反して起こることをめったに恐れない」

④ 「世の中が私たちに報いてくれると期待すべきだ」

▶ 第1段落最終文，最終段落第2文参照。

（エ）「ローバー・バーンズが言おうとしていることは_____ということである」

① 「私たちは最善の計画を立てれば生活を向上させることができる」

57

② 「私たちは不運だと哀れな生活を送らなければならないことが多い」

③ **「最善の計画でさえ悲しくて痛ましい結果になりかねない」**

④ 「最善の計画があれば私たちは落胆せずにすむだろう」

▶ 第3段落最終文参照。

(オ) 「この文章に最も適切なタイトルは＿＿＿である」

① 「人生は必ずしも公平ではない」

② 「他人の感情を受け止める方法」

③ 「人はどんなときでも愛情豊かで忠実でいられるわけではない」

④ **「物事は必ずしも計画通りに進行するわけではない」**

▶ ④の内容は第1段落最終文，第2段落最終文，第4段落第2文などに書かれている。

▼

それでは次に，段落ごとに詳しくみていこう。

23

第1段落 文の構造と語句のチェック

¹(In the early 1940s), (on the night of her graduation party), <u>a high school</u>
S

<u>girl</u> 〔named Doris Van Kappelhoff〕 <u>was involved</u> (in a serious car accident).
V

²<u>She</u> <u>had planned to go</u> (to Hollywood) (to become a dancer in films), but
S V 等接

<u>her injuries</u> <u>made</u> <u>that future</u> <u>no longer possible.</u> ³(During her long recovery 〔 at
S V O C

home 〕), <u>Doris</u> <u>began to sing</u> (along with the female vocalists 〔 on the radio 〕).
S V

⁴<u>Her voice</u> <u>became</u> so <u>well trained</u> that <u>she</u> <u>was hired</u> (to sing in a band), and
S V C S V 等接

(soon thereafter), <u>she</u> <u>found</u> <u>parts</u> 〔 in movies 〕, (<u>changing</u> <u>her name</u> to Doris
S V O V' O'

Day).　⁵Her original plans were destroyed (by a tragic event), but thereby she
　　　　　　S　　　　　　　　V　　　　　　　　　　　　　　　　　　等接　　　　S

found her true calling.　⁶Things don't always go (according to our plans), but
　V　　　O　　　　　　　　　　S　　　　　　　V　　　　　　　　　　　　　　　　等接

a change of plans may be an example 〔 of coincidental circumstances 〔 that lead
　　　S　　　　　　V　　　C　　　　　　　　　　　　　　　　　　　　　　関代　V

us (to a fulfilling life, 〔 unguessed and unsought 〕— a blessing from God)〕〕.
O　　①　　　　　　　　　等接②　　　　　　　　　　└─同格─┘

訳　¹1940年代はじめ，卒業パーティーの日の夜，ドリス・ヴァン・カッペルホフという名前の女子高校生が重大な自動車事故に巻き込まれた。²彼女は映画に出るダンサーになるためにハリウッドに行くことを計画していたのだが，負傷のせいで，もはやその将来は不可能になってしまった。³回復するまでの自宅での長い期間，ドリスはラジオの女性歌手たちと一緒に歌い始めた。⁴彼女の声は非常に良く訓練されたものになったため，雇われてバンドで歌うようになり，その後すぐに映画での配役をもらい，名前もドリス・デイに改めた。⁵彼女の当初の計画は悲劇的な出来事によって打ち砕かれてしまったが，それによって彼女は本当の天職を見出したのだ。⁶物事は必ずしも計画どおりに進むわけではないが，計画の変更は，私たちを予想も期待もしていなかった充実した人生――神様からの恵み――に導いてくれるような偶然の出来事の一例となるかもしれないのだ。

Check!　第6文 Things don't always go according to our plans, … の not always は
「必ずしも～ではない，いつも～とは限らない」の意味で，【部分否定】を表す。

語句

graduation	名	卒業	vocalist	名 歌手
be involved in ~	熟	～に巻き込まれている	voice	名 声
serious	形	深刻な，重大な	trained	形 訓練された，熟練した
plan to *do*	熟	～しようと計画する	hire	動 雇う
film	名	映画	band	名 バンド，楽団
injury	名	けが，負傷	thereafter	副 その後
future	名	将来，未来	part	名 (劇などの)役，配役
no longer	熟	もはや～ない	original	形 最初の，本来の
recovery	名	回復	destroy	動 壊す，打ち砕く
along with ~	熟	～とともに，～と一緒に	tragic	形 悲劇的な
female	形	女性の	event	名 出来事，事件
			thereby	副 それにより

calling	名 職業, 天職	circumstance	名 状況, 出来事
not always	熟 必ずしも〜ではない, いつも〜とは限らない	lead *A* to *B*	熟 A を B に導く
according to 〜		fulfilling	形 充実した, やりがいのある
	熟 〜にしたがって, 〜のとおりに	unguessed	形 予期できない, 思いもよらない
example	名 例	unsought	形 望んでいない
coincidental	形 偶然の	blessing	名 (神の)恵み

第2段落 文の構造と語句のチェック

¹We make plans (expecting to be in control of what will happen). ²Perhaps
　　S　　V　　O

we fear natural happenings, things 〔 turning out contrary (to our wishes)〕.
　S　V　　　　O　　└─同格─┘　　V′　　　　C′

³The course of life is challenging (if we are concerned (with trying to control
　　　　S　　　　　V　　C　　従接 S　V　　C

it)). ⁴We may act (with precision, and self-discipline), (expecting the world to
　　　　S　　V　　　　①　　等接　　②　　　　V′　　O′

① 　　　　等接 ② 　　　　関代
do the same and give us 〈 what we want 〉), but that is rarely the case.
　　　　C′　　　　　　　　　　　　　等接 S V　　　C

> **訳** ¹私たちは将来起こることをコントロールしようと期待して計画を立てる。²もしかすると私たちは自然の出来事, つまり, 物事が結局自分の希望に反することを恐れているのかもしれない。³人生の進路は, 私たちが人生をコントロールしようとすることに関心があると, 困難なものとなる。⁴私たちは世間が(自分と)同じことをし, 欲しいものを与えてくれると期待して, 正確さと自制心をもって行動するかもしれないが, そのようなことはめったにないのである。

Check! 第4文 We may act with precision, and self-discipline, expecting the world to do the same and give us what we want, ... の expecting は【付帯状況】を表す分詞構文。「〜して, 〜しながら」などと訳す。

60

語句

expect	動	予期する，期待する

▶ expect＋O＋to *do*
　　　　　　熟 Oが〜することを予期[期待]する

in control of 〜　熟 〜を支配[管理，制御]して

perhaps　副 ひょっとすると，もしかすると

happening　名 (思いがけない)出来事

turn out (to be) 〜
　　　　熟 結局〜になる，結局〜だとわかる

contrary to 〜　熟 〜と反対の，〜に反する

course　名 進路，方向

challenging　形 困難な，苦労を伴う

be concerned with 〜
　　　　　　熟 〜に関心を持っている

try to *do*　熟 〜しようと試みる

act　動 行動する，ふるまう

precision　名 正確さ，精度

self-discipline　名 自己鍛錬，自制(心)

rarely　副 めったに〜ない

be the case　熟 事実である，あてはまる

第3段落　文の構造と語句のチェック

¹Perfect discipline, or perfect control, is the most certain way〔to miss out on
　S①　　　　　等接　　　S②　　　V　　　C

the joy of life〕. ²The unexpectedness of life means〈that we are free（not to
　　　　　　　　　　　　　　S　　　　　　V　O 従接　S　V　C

plan perfectly）〉. ³We can flow（into the natural chaos of life, so untidy, so
　　　　　　　　　　S　　V

unpredictable）, or we can try to order life fully（by making careful plans）.
　　　　　　　　　　等接　S　　　V　　　O　　　　　　V′　　　O′

⁴But（as Rover Burns says）, "The best-prepared schemes often go wrong and
等接　従接　S　　　V　　　　　　S　　　　　　　　　　V①　C　等接

leave us nothing but grief and pain〔for promised joy〕."
V②　O₁　　　　　　　　O₂

訳 ¹完璧な統制，すなわち完璧なコントロールは，人生の喜びを逃してしまう最も確実な方法である。²人生の意外性とは，完全に計画を立てない自由があるということを意味する。³私たちは，非常に雑然として予測不可能な，人生の自然のままの混沌状態の中へ流れ込んでいくこともできるし，あるいは慎重な計画を立てることにより人生を完全に律しようとすることもできる。⁴しかし，ローバー・バーンズが述べているように，「最も用意周到な計画はしばしば失敗に終わり，私たちに残されるのは約束されていたはずの喜びに対する悲嘆と苦痛だけなのである」。

Check! 最終文 … and leave us nothing but grief and pain for promised joy の leave は SVOO の文型。〈leave＋O_1＋O_2〉で「O_1 に O_2 を残す」。ここでは us が O_1, nothing 〜 joy が O_2 となる。

語句

discipline	名	規律，統制	order	動	整える，整理する	
certain	形	確実な	**fully**	副	完全に，十分に	
miss out on 〜	熟	〜(の機会)を逃す	well-prepared	形	準備万端な，用意周到な	
unexpectedness	名	予想外であること	**scheme**	名	計画	
be free to _do_	熟	自由に〜できる	**go wrong**	熟	うまくいかなくなる，失敗する	
flow into 〜	熟	〜に流れ込む	**nothing but 〜**	熟	〜だけ，〜のみ	
chaos	名	混沌，大混乱	**grief**	名	悲しみ	
untidy	形	乱れて，雑然として	**pain**	名	苦痛	
unpredictable	形	予測不可能な	**promise**	動	約束する	
			joy	名	喜び	

第4段落　文の構造と語句のチェック

¹〈 Making plans 〉is an adult occupation, a feature of a healthy ego. ²However,
　　S　　　　　　　V　　C　　　└─同格─┘

life often does not proceed (according to our plans). ³This does not
S　　　　V　　　　　　　　　　　　　　　　　　　　S

── 従接 that 省略

have to leave us disappointed. ⁴Perhaps we believe 〈 the universe has a plan
　　　V　　O　C　　　　　　　S　V　　O　S　　V　O

〔 that more accurately reflects our emerging destiny 〕〉.
　関代　　　　　　V　　　　O

訳 ¹計画を立てることは大人の仕事であり，健全な自意識の特徴である。²しかし，人生は計画どおりに進まないことが多い。³そうだからといって私たちはがっかりする必要はない。⁴もしかすると私たちは，明らかになりつつある私たちの運命をより正確に反映する計画がこの世界にあるのだと，思い込んでいるのかもしれない。

Check! 第3文 This does not have to leave us disappointed. の leave は SVOC の文型。〈leave＋O＋C〉で「O を C の状態(のまま)にしておく」の意味。

62

語句

adult	形 大人の，大人びた	disappointed	形 がっかりして，失望して
occupation	名 仕事	universe	名 宇宙，全世界
feature	名 特徴，特色	accurately	副 正確に
healthy	形 健全な，自然な	reflect	動 反映する
ego	名 自意識，自尊心	emerge	動 現れる，明らかになる
proceed	動 進む，進行する	destiny	名 運命，宿命

文法事項の整理 ⑤ 無生物主語

第 1 段落第 2 文の無生物主語についてみてみよう。

..., but **her injuries** made that future no longer possible.

　主語が人間ではなく物事の場合，【**無生物主語**】という。そのような英文はいくらでもあるが，問題となるのは，直訳が不自然な場合である。たとえば，次のような訳は，明らかに不自然である。

例 The heavy rain prevented us from going out.
　（直訳）「大雨が私たちを外出することから妨げた」
そこで，「大雨のせいで私たちは外出できなかった」などと訳す。
以上を整理すると，次のようになる。

無生物主語（＝S が物事）

　直訳は不自然！　→　①英文の S を副詞的に訳す。
　　　　　　　　　　　②可能な限り，人が主体となるように訳す。

---

①においては，どのように「副詞的に」訳すのかを押さえておこう。

■無生物主語の訳し方

	過去～現在	現在～未来
肯定文	(1) **because**	(3) **if**
否定文	(2) **though**	(4) **even if**

以下の例文で確認しよう（番号は表中のものと対応）。

(1) Hard work enabled him to succeed.

（直訳）「一生懸命働くことは，彼が成功することを可能にした」

▸ 過去形・肯定文なので **because** のイメージで訳す。

（意訳）「一生懸命働いたので，彼は成功できた」

(2) Hard work didn't enable him to succeed.

（直訳）「一生懸命働くことは，彼が成功することを可能にしなかった」

▸ 過去形・否定文なので **though** のイメージで訳す。

（意訳）「一生懸命働いたのだが，彼は成功できなかった」

(3) Hard work will enable him to succeed.

（直訳）「一生懸命働くことは，彼が成功することを可能にするだろう」

▸ 未来形・肯定文なので **if** のイメージで訳す。

（意訳）「もし一生懸命働けば，彼は成功できるだろう」

(4) Hard work won't enable him to succeed.

（直訳）「一生懸命働くことは，彼が成功することを可能にしないだろう」

▸ 未来形・否定文なので **even if** のイメージで訳す。

（意訳）「たとえ一生懸命働いても，彼は成功できないだろう」

■第1段落第2文

..., but her injuries made that future no longer possible.

▸ 直訳すれば「彼女の負傷はそのような将来をもはや不可能にした」。前のページの表の(1)より，**because** のイメージで訳すと「彼女が負傷したため[負傷のせいで]，そのような将来はもはや不可能となってしまった」となる。

■第4段落第3文

This does not have to leave us disappointed.

▸ 直訳すれば「このことは私たちをがっかりさせておく必要はない」。表の(2)より，**though** のイメージで訳すと「そうであるが，私たちはがっかりする必要はない」となる。また，(4)より，**even if** のイメージで訳すと「たとえそうだとしても，私たちはがっかりする必要はない」となる（※時制が現在の場合は，表の左右いずれの訳も可能。文脈に応じて適したほうを選ぶ）。

確認問題

/40点

1. 次の和訳と対応する英語の語句を，頭文字を参考にして書き，空欄を完成させよう。

(各1点×20)

①	g		名	卒業
② be	i	i ~	熟	~に巻き込まれている
③	i		名	けが，負傷
④	r		名	回復
⑤	h		動	雇う
⑥	o		形	最初の，本来の
⑦	t		形	悲劇的な
⑧	c		名	職業，天職
⑨	a	t ~	熟	~にしたがって，~のとおりに
⑩	c		名	状況，出来事
⑪	c	t ~	熟	~と反対の，~に反する
⑫ be	c	w ~	熟	~に関心を持っている
⑬	d		名	規律，統制
⑭	f		副	完全に，十分に
⑮	s		名	計画
⑯	n	b ~	熟	~だけ，~のみ
⑰	g		名	悲しみ
⑱	f		名	特徴，特色
⑲	a		副	正確に
⑳	d		名	運命，宿命

2. 次の [ ] 内の語句を並べ替えて，意味の通る英文を完成させよう。(各5点×2)

① Things [always / our / don't / according / plans / go / to].

② The best-prepared schemes often go wrong and [but / us / leave / grief /

nothing] and pain for promised joy.

3. 次の英文を和訳してみよう。(10点)

She had planned to go to Hollywood to become a dancer in films, but her injuries made that future no longer possible.

ディクテーションしてみよう！

今回学習した英文に出てきた語句・表現を，＿＿＿に書き取ろう。

24　In the early 1940s, on the night of her graduation party, a high school girl named Doris Van Kappelhoff was ❶＿＿＿＿＿＿＿＿＿＿ a serious car accident.　She had planned to go to Hollywood to become a dancer in films, but her injuries made that future no longer possible. During her long recovery at home, Doris began to sing along with the female vocalists on the radio.　Her voice became so well trained that she was hired to ❷＿＿＿＿＿＿＿＿＿＿＿, and soon thereafter, she found parts in movies, changing her name to Doris Day.　Her original plans were destroyed by a tragic event, but thereby she found ❸＿＿＿＿＿＿＿＿＿＿＿. Things don't always go according to our plans, but a change of plans may be an example of coincidental circumstances that lead us to a fulfilling life, unguessed and unsought — ❹＿＿＿＿＿＿＿＿＿＿ God.

25　We make plans ❺＿＿＿＿＿＿＿＿＿ be in control of what will happen.　Perhaps we fear natural happenings, things turning out contrary to our wishes.　The course of life is challenging if we are concerned with trying to control it.　We may act with precision, and self-discipline, expecting the world to do the same and give us what we want, but that is ❻＿＿＿＿＿＿＿＿＿＿＿.

26　Perfect discipline, or perfect control, is the most certain way to ❼＿＿＿＿＿＿＿＿ the joy of life.　The unexpectedness of life means that we are free not to plan perfectly.　We can flow into the natural chaos of life, so untidy, so unpredictable, or we can try to order life fully by making careful plans. But as Rover Burns says, "The best-prepared schemes often go wrong and ❽_____ grief and pain for promised joy."

27 Making plans is ❾_____, a feature of a healthy ego. However, life often does not proceed according to our plans. This does not have to leave us disappointed. Perhaps we believe the universe has a plan that ❿_____ reflects our emerging destiny.

確認問題の答 1. ① graduation　② involved in　③ injury　④ recovery　⑤ hire
⑥ original　⑦ tragic　⑧ calling　⑨ according to　⑩ circumstance
⑪ contrary to　⑫ concerned with　⑬ discipline　⑭ fully　⑮ scheme
⑯ nothing but　⑰ grief　⑱ feature　⑲ accurately　⑳ destiny

2. ① don't always go according to our plans　（第1段落　最終文）
② leave us nothing but grief　（第3段落　最終文）

3. 彼女は映画に出るダンサーになるためにハリウッドに行くことを計画していたのだが，負傷のせいで，もはやその将来は不可能になってしまった。（第1段落　第2文）

ディクテーションしてみよう！の答　❶ involved in　❷ sing in a band　❸ her true calling
❹ a blessing from　❺ expecting to　❻ rarely the case　❼ miss out on
❽ leave us nothing but　❾ an adult occupation　❿ more accurately

アドバイス ❼ miss の /s/ の音と後ろの out の /a/ の音がつながり「サ」のように聞こえる（⇒連結）。また，/t/ や /d/ の音が母音に挟まれると，「ら行」のような音になる（⇒フラッピング）ので，out の /t/ と後ろの on は「ロン」のようになる。miss out on 全体としては，「ミサウロン」のように聞こえる。

解 答

問1	(ア)	①	(イ)	③	(ウ)	②
問2	(エ)	④	(オ)	②	(カ)	①

解 説

問1

(ア) in order to *do* で「～するために」の意味。【目的】を表す。なお、②の with regard to ～ や④の with reference to ～ は「～に関して」の意味だが、「～」の部分は名詞なので、ここでは文法的にも不可。

(イ) on the contrary は**「それどころか」**の意味で、前の内容を修正して言い直すときに使う。

> 例　The results were not bad; <u>on the contrary</u>, they showed great improvement.
> 「結果は悪くなかった。それどころか、大幅な改善が見られた」

ここでは、「問題はない→それどころか→好印象で有利になる」という流れ。他の選択肢の意味は、①「しかし」、②「さらに、その上」、④「その結果」。

(ウ) 好印象を与えるための条件を列挙している文脈。直後の文に It is also very important ... とあるので、**(ウ)**を含む文はこれと類似した内容になるはず。② essential は「非常に重要な、必要不可欠な」（≒very important）という意味で、これが正解。他の選択肢の意味は、①「正式な」、③「純粋な、本物の」、④「正当な、有効な」。

問2

(エ) 「就職活動に関する本は＿＿＿＿＿＿」
① 「読むのがつらい」
② 「雇用者になりそうな人を列挙している」
③ 「人々を緊張させる」
④ **「役に立つ手引きを与えてくれる」**
▶ ④が第1段落第2、3文と一致。

（オ）「求職者は＿＿＿＿＿＿すべきだ」

① 「事前に到着した場合，何者か知られるのを避ける」

② **「道に迷うのを避けるため1日早くオフィスを訪れる」**

③ 「頭が良いと思われるために，約束の時間を過ぎてから到着する」

④ 「従業員の衣服や行動について自分の考えを述べる」

▶ ②が第2段落第3文と一致。

（カ）「良い第一印象を与えることは重要である。なぜなら＿＿＿＿＿＿からだ」

① **「管理職の人は採用の決断を非常に素早く行う」**

② 「志願者はちゃんとした服装をし，興味を持っている」

③ 「面接官は誠実な『アイコンタクト』に印象付けられる」

④ 「志願者はその他の点では良くない反応をする」

▶ ①が第3段落第1文と一致。③については第3段落最終文に「目を見ること」が重要である理由として挙げられている。

それでは次に，段落ごとに詳しくみていこう。

第1段落　文の構造と語句のチェック

¹〈 Hunting for a job 〉 is a painful experience, but one 〔 that nearly everyone
　　S　　　　　　　　　 V　　　 C①　　　　　 等接　C②　 関代　　　　　S

must endure (at least once) (in a lifetime)〕.　²Books are published and
　V　　　　　　　　　　　　　　　　　　　　　　　　　　S　 V　　　　　 等接

magazine articles are written (on the subject), (all trying to tell job-seekers
　　S　　　　　　　　　 V　　　　　　　　　　　　　 S′　 V′　　　　　 O₁′

┌── should 省略
〈 what they should do or avoid doing (in order to survive and to win the game)〉〉).
O₂′ 疑　 S　　 V①　 等接 V②　 O　　　　　 ①　　　 等接　　②

³They can't calm the nervous applicant ((and what applicant is not nervous?),
　S　 V　　　　 O　　　　　　　　　　　 等接　　　 S　　　 V　 O

but they do offer some advice〔that deserves consideration〕.
等接　S　V　　　O　　　　関代　　V　　　　O

> **訳** ¹就職活動は苦痛な経験であるが，ほぼすべての人が一生に少なくとも一度は耐えなくてはならない経験である。²そのテーマに関して様々な本が出版され，雑誌の記事が書かれており，いずれも求職者に対し，生き残ってゲームに勝つためには，何をすべきか，あるいは何をするのを避けるべきかを伝えようとしている。³それらは緊張している求職者を落ち着かせることはできない（そして，どんな応募者が緊張していないというのだろうか）が，考慮に値する助言を実際に提供してくれているのだ。

Check! 第1文 Hunting for a job is a painful experience, but one that nearly everyone must endure at least once in a lifetime. の one は an experience の代用となる代名詞。that は目的格の関係代名詞で，endure の後に O が欠けている。

語句

hunt for ~	熟	~を探し求める
painful	形	つらい，苦痛な
experience	名	経験
nearly	副	ほとんど，ほぼ
endure	動	耐える，我慢する
at least	熟	少なくとも
lifetime	名	一生，生涯
publish	動	出版する
article	名	記事
subject	名	主題，テーマ

job-seeker	名	求職者，就職希望者
avoid	動	避ける
in order to *do*	熟	~するために
survive	動	生き残る
calm	動	落ち着かせる，なだめる
nervous	形	緊張して
applicant	名	応募者，志願者
offer	動	提供する
deserve	動	値する
consideration	名	考慮

第2段落　文の構造と語句のチェック

¹(To begin with), it is not a good idea 〈 to be late 〉. ²Job interviewers
　　　　　　　　　仮S　V　　　C　　　真S　　　　　　　　　　　S

don't think very highly of the candidate〔who arrives (twenty minutes after the
　　V　　　　　　　　　　O　　　　　関代　V

appointed time), (① offering no apology) or (② explaining 〔that he couldn't find
　　　　　　　　　　　V′　　O′　　等接　　　V′　　O′①　S　　V
　　　　　　　　　　　　　　　　　　　　　　　　　　従接

70

the street 〉, and 〈 that his watch is slow 〉)〕. ³The wise job-seeker explores
　　　　O　　　　等接 O'②   従接   S　　V　C　　　　　　　　S　　　　　　V

the place (the day before) (to make sure 〈 that he can locate the building,
　　O　　　　　　　　　　　　　　　V'　　O' 従接 S　　V　　　O①

the right floor, and the office 〔in which the interview is to take place 〕〉); (at
　　O②　　　　等接　　O③　　関代　　　　　S　　　　V

the same time) he looks around (to see 〈 what the employees are wearing 〉 and
　　　　　　　　　S　　V　　　　　V'　O①　　　　S　　　　V　　　等接

〈 how they seem to behave (at work)〉). ⁴(Next day) he arrives (early for the
O'②　　S　　V　　　　　　　　　　　　　　　　　S　　V

appointment). ⁵It does not matter (if the employer's secretary recognizes him
　　　　　　　　　S　　V　　　従接　　　　S　　　　V①　　O

and mentions his first visit (to her boss)). ⁶(On the contrary), the eager
等接　V②　　　O　　　　　　　　　　　　　　　　　　　　　　　　　　

candidate can only be regarded (as smart, thoughtful, and well-organized) —
　　S　　　　V　　　　　　　①　　　②　　等接　　③

three points in his favor (before he has said a word).
　　　　　　　　　　　　　　従接　S　V　　O

> **訳** ¹まず第一に，遅刻をするのは良い考えではない。²就職の面接官は，約束の時間の20分後に到着し，謝罪もせず，あるいは道がわからなかったとか時計が遅れていたなどと釈明をするような志願者のことは，あまり高く評価しない。³賢明な求職者は前日に，面接が行われる予定の建物，正しい階，オフィスを確実に見つけられるよう，現地を調査する。同時に，従業員が何を着ているか，そして彼らが仕事中にどのような行動をしているように思われるかを確かめるために，見て回る。⁴翌日は約束のために早めに到着する。⁵雇用者の秘書がその人に見覚えがあって，最初の訪問について上司に言ったとしても問題ない。⁶それどころか，その熱意ある志願者は，頭が良く，思慮深く，几帳面であると見てもらえるだけである。つまり，一言も発しないうちに３つの点が有利に働くのだ。

Check! 第３文 ... and the office in which the interview is to take place の is to は「～する予定である」の意味。be to do は【義務】【予定】【運命】【可能】【意図】などの意味を持つ。

第5文 It does not matter if the employer's secretary recognizes him ... の if は副詞節を導き，「たとえ…しても」（≒even if）の意味。It は形式主語（仮主語）ではなく，後続の if 節の内容を指す。

例 I'd appreciate it if you would help me.
「手伝っていただけるならありがたいのですが」

語句

to begin with	熟	最初に，まず第一に
interviewer	名	面接官，面接担当者
think highly of ~	熟	~を高く評価する，~を重視する
candidate	名	志願者，志望者
appointed	形	指定された，約束の
apology	名	謝罪
explain	動	説明する
explore	動	調査する
the day before	熟	前日（に）
make sure that ...	熟	…ということを確認する，確実にする
locate	動	（場所を）見つける
interview	名	面接
take place	熟	行われる，起こる
at the same time	熟	同時に
look around	熟	周囲を見回す，見て回る
employee	名	従業員

seem to *do*	熟	~するように思われる
behave	動	ふるまう，行動する
at work	熟	仕事中に，職場で
appointment	名	（面会の）約束，予約
matter	動	重要である，問題となる
employer	名	雇い主，雇用者
secretary	名	秘書
recognize	動	（人の）顔を覚えている，見覚えがある
mention	動	言及する，述べる
boss	名	上司
on the contrary	熟	それどころか，反対に
eager	形	熱心な，熱意のある
regard *A* as *B*	熟	A を B とみなす
smart	形	賢明な，頭の良い
thoughtful	形	思慮深い
well-organized	形	（人が）きちんとした，几帳面な
in *one*'s favor	熟	~に有利で

第3段落 文の構造と語句のチェック

[1]Most personnel managers admit 〈 that they know （ within the first few
　　S　　　　　　　　V　O 従接　S　V

minutes of the meeting 〉〈 whether or not they want to hire the person 〔 to
　　　　　　　　　　　　　　O　従接　　　　　S　　V　　　　　　O

whom they are talking 〕〉〉. [2]This is particularly true (when their first reaction
関代　S　　V　　　　　　　　　　S　V　　　C　　　　　　従接　　　their first reaction
　　　　　　　　　　　　　　　　　　　　　　　　　　　　　　　　　　　　　S

〔 to the applicant 〕 is negative ），（ when the man or woman has made a
               V   C   従接   S   V

disastrous first impression ）． ³But what makes a *good* impression? ⁴What
              O   等接 S   V   O   S

counts? ⁵〈 Being on time 〉 does, （ as we have seen ）; then, appearance. ⁶It is
  V   S   V   従接 S   V   S   仮S V

does 省略 →

essential 〈 for the candidate to be dressed properly, and to look alert,
  C   真S   S′   V′①   等接 V′②

pleasant, and interested 〉． ⁷It is also very important 〈 to look the interviewer
   C′   等接 ③   仮S V   C   真S V′   O′

（ in the eyes ）〉（ because this "eye contact" gives a strong impression 〔 of
           従接   S   V   O

sincerity and openness 〕）．
  ①   等接   ②

訳 ¹ほとんどの人事部長は，会ってから最初の数分以内に，自分が話している人物を採用したいかどうかわかると認める。²これは，応募者に対する最初の反応が良くなかったり，その男性または女性がひどい第一印象を与えてしまった場合には，特にそうである。³しかし，何が「良い」印象を作り出すのだろうか。⁴何が重要なのだろうか。⁵ここまでに見てきたように，時間に正確であるということは，確かにあてはまる。次に，外見である。⁶志願者は適切な服装をし，機敏で愛想が良く興味を持っているように見えることが不可欠である。⁷また，面接官の目をしっかり見ることも非常に重要である。なぜなら，こういう「アイコンタクト」は誠実で心が広いという強い印象を与えるからだ。

Check! 第 1 文 … they know within the first few minutes of the meeting whether or not they want to hire the person to whom they are talking. の V が know，O は whether 以下。この場合の whether は名詞節の用法で「…かどうか」の意味。V と O の間に前置詞句（within the first few minutes of the meeting）が挟まっている。なお，whether の後の or not は節の最後に置くこともあり，省略可能で，なくても意味は変わらない。

Check! 第 5 文の does は代動詞で，第 4 文の counts の代用。appearance の後にも同様の does が省略されていると考えてよい。

personnel	名 人事(部)	**count**	動 重要である
manager	名 部長，主任	**appearance**	名 外見
admit	動 認める	**essential**	形 必要不可欠の，重要な
within	前 ～のうちに，範囲内で	**dress**	動 衣服を身につける
hire	動 雇う	**properly**	副 適切に
particularly	副 特に	**alert**	形 油断のない，機敏な
reaction	名 反応	**pleasant**	形 愛想の良い，好感の持てる
negative	形 否定的な，マイナスの	**look ～ in the eye(s)**	
disastrous	形 ひどい，悲惨な		熟 ～(人)の目をじっと見る
impression	名 印象	**sincerity**	名 誠実さ，誠意
		openness	名 心の広さ，開放性

文法事項の整理 ⑥　強調の do

第 1 段落最終文の do についてみてみよう。

..., but they **do** offer some advice that deserves consideration.

〈do [does / did]＋原形〉は動詞の【強調】を表す。「確かに，実際，本当に（～する）」などと訳す。また，命令文の場合は「ぜひ～しなさい」と訳す。

例　He *does* understand what you said.
「彼はあなたが言ったことをちゃんと理解していますよ」

例　"You didn't say that." "I *did* say that!"
「君はそんなことは言わなかったよ」「いや，確かに言った！」

例　*Do* come to see us.
「ぜひ会いにいらっしゃい」

■第 1 段落最終文

..., but they do offer some advice that deserves consideration.

▶ do が直後の動詞 offer を強調している。

確認問題

/40点

1. 次の和訳と対応する英語の語句を，頭文字を参考にして書き，空欄を完成させよう。

（各1点×20）

①	p	形	つらい，苦痛な
②	e	名	経験
③	e	動	耐える，我慢する
④	p	動	出版する
⑤	a	名	記事
⑥	s	形	主題，テーマ
⑦	a	名	応募者，志願者
⑧	c	名	考慮
⑨	a	名	謝罪
⑩	e	動	調査する
⑪	i	名	面接
⑫	a	名	(面会の)約束，予約
⑬	s	名	秘書
⑭	m	動	言及する，述べる
⑮	s	形	賢明な，頭の良い
⑯	a	動	認める
⑰	r	名	反応
⑱	a	名	外見
⑲	e	形	必要不可欠の，重要な
⑳	s	名	誠実さ，誠意

2. 次の[　]内の語句を並べ替えて，意味の通る英文を完成させよう。（各5点×2）

① Job interviewers [of / very / the / think / candidate / don't / highly] who arrives twenty minutes after the appointed time.

② It is [to / for / candidate / dressed / essential / the / be] properly, and to look alert, pleasant, and interested.

3. 次の英文を和訳してみよう。（10点）

Hunting for a job is a painful experience, but one that nearly everyone must endure at least once in a lifetime.

ディクテーションしてみよう！

今回学習した英文に出てきた語句・表現を，＿＿＿に書き取ろう。

29　Hunting for a job is a painful experience, but one that nearly everyone ❶_____ at least once in a lifetime. Books are published and magazine articles are written on the subject, all trying to tell job-seekers what they should do or avoid doing in order to survive and to win the game. They can't calm the nervous applicant (and what applicant is not nervous?), but they do offer some advice that ❷_____.

30　To begin with, it is not a good idea to be late. Job interviewers don't think very highly of the candidate who arrives twenty minutes after the ❸_____, offering no apology or explaining that he couldn't find the street, and that his watch is slow. The wise job-seeker explores the place the day before to make sure that he can locate the building, the right floor, and the office in which the interview is ❹_____ _____; at the same time he looks around to see what the employees are wearing and how they seem to behave at work. Next day he arrives early for the appointment. It ❺_____ if the employer's secretary recognizes him and mentions his first visit to her boss. On the contrary, the eager candidate can only be regarded as smart, thoughtful, and well-organized — three points ❻_____ before he has said a word.

31 Most personnel managers ❼_____ they know within the first few minutes of the meeting whether or not they want to hire the person to whom they are talking. This is particularly true when their first reaction to the applicant is negative, when the man or woman has made a disastrous first impression. But what makes a *good* impression? ❽_____ _____? Being on time does, as we have seen; then, appearance. It is essential for the candidate to ❾_____, and to look alert, pleasant, and interested. It is also very important to look the interviewer ❿_____ because this "eye contact" gives a strong impression of sincerity and openness.

確認問題の答 **1.** ① painful   ② experience   ③ endure   ④ publish   ⑤ article
⑥ subject   ⑦ applicant   ⑧ consideration   ⑨ apology   ⑩ explore
⑪ interview   ⑫ appointment   ⑬ secretary   ⑭ mention   ⑮ smart
⑯ admit   ⑰ reaction   ⑱ appearance   ⑲ essential   ⑳ sincerity

2. ① don't think very highly of the candidate （第2段落　第2文）
② essential for the candidate to be dressed （第3段落　第6文）

3. 就職活動は苦痛な経験であるが，ほぼすべての人が一生に少なくとも一度は耐えなくてはならない経験である。 （第1段落　第1文）

ディクテーションしてみよう！の答 ❶ must endure   ❷ deserves consideration
❸ appointed time   ❹ to take place   ❺ does not matter   ❻ in his favor
❼ admit that   ❽ What counts   ❾ be dressed properly   ❿ in the eyes

アドバイス ❺ /t/ や /d/ の音が母音に挟まれると「ら行」のような音になる（⇒フラッピング）。matter は「マター」というより「マラ」のように聞こえる。

❼同じ子音，または発音の仕方が似た子音が2つ続く場合，前の子音がほとんど発音されなくなる（⇒脱落）。admit の /t/ と that の /ð/ もこのタイプなので，/t/ がほとんど発音されない。

解 答

問1	(ア)	②	(イ)	②	(ウ)	①	(エ)	①	(オ)	③
問2	①	×	②	○	③	○	④	×	⑤	×

解 説

問1

(ア) 選択肢は，① steam「蒸す，ふかす」，② grind「すりつぶす，粉にする」，③ peel「(皮を)むく」。目的語が corn(小麦などの穀物)であり，風力を使うということから判断する。また，直後の部分で windmill「風車」という語の語源になっているとの記述があり，mill は「製粉所」の意味なので，これもヒントになる。

(イ)「てっぺんにプロペラがついている塔」という意味にするのが自然。with は「～のある，～がついている」という【付属・存在】の意味をもつ。

(ウ) 目的語が many of these towers である点，副詞の together「(同じ場所に)一緒に，まとめて」があることから考える。

(エ) at the top(s) of ～ で「～のてっぺん[頂上]に」の意味。at は【点・地点】を表す前置詞。

(オ) farms「農場」は Isolated places「孤立した場所」の具体例。***A such as B* [such *A* as *B*]「Bのような A」**において，B は A の具体例となる。

問2

① 「ヨーロッパ人が初めて農業において風力を利用した」

▶ 第1段落第2, 3文と不一致。the Middle Ages「中世」のヨーロッパ人よりも 4,000 年前のバビロニア人や中国人の方が古い。

② **「風が起こる原因は空気中の場所によって気温が異なることにある」**

▶ 第2段落第1, 2文と一致。

③ **「風力発電地帯は，風がより強い場所に建設される」**

▶ 第2段落最終文と一致。

④ 「ほとんどの風力発電地帯は沖合にある」

▶ 第3段落第2文と不一致。「ほとんど」とは書かれていない。

⑤「垂直のタービンは風の方を向くように発電機とプロペラを回転させる」

▶ 第4段落第2, 3文と不一致。

それでは次に, 段落ごとに詳しくみていこう。

32

第1段落 文の構造と語句のチェック

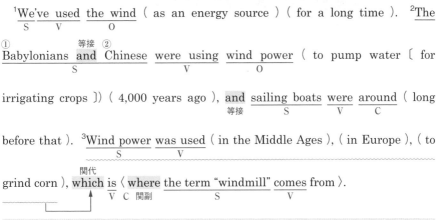

¹We've used the wind (as an energy source) (for a long time). ²The Babylonians and Chinese were using wind power (to pump water 〔 for irrigating crops 〕) (4,000 years ago), and sailing boats were around (long before that). ³Wind power was used (in the Middle Ages), (in Europe), (to grind corn), which is 〈 where the term "windmill" comes from 〉.

訳 ¹私たちは長い間, 風をエネルギー源として使ってきた。²バビロニア人や中国人は4,000年前に農作物のかんがい用の水をくみ上げるのに風力を使っていたし, 帆船はそのずっと前からあった。³中世のヨーロッパでも風力は穀物を粉にするために使われており, それがwindmill（風車）という語の由来である。

Check! 第3文 Wind power was used in the Middle Ages, in Europe, to grind corn, which is where the term "windmill" comes from. の which は【非制限用法】の関係代名詞。主節全体の内容を受ける用法（→ p.95 参照）。また where は関係副詞で, 先行詞が省略されている。

第2段落 文の構造と語句のチェック

¹The sun heats our atmosphere unevenly, so some parts become warmer
（S）（V）（O）（等接）（S）（V）（C）

(than others). ²These warm parts rise up, other air blows in (to replace them)
（S）（V）（S）（V）

— and we feel a wind blowing. ³We can use the energy 〔 in the wind 〕 (by
（等接）（S）（V）（O）（C）（S）（V）（O）

building a tall tower, 〔 with a large propeller on the top 〕). ⁴The wind blows
（S）（V）

the propeller round, which turns a generator (to produce electricity). ⁵We
（O）（関代）（V）（O）（S）

tend to build many of these towers together, (to make a "wind farm" and
（V）（O）（V①）（O）（等接）

there are 省略 / there is 省略
produce more electricity). ⁶(The more towers, the more wind, and the larger
（V②）（O）（S）（S）（等接）（C）

are 省略
the propellers), the more electricity we can make. ⁷It's only worth 〈 building
（S）（O）（S）（V）（仮S）（V）（C）（真S）（V'）

wind farms (in places 〔 that have strong, steady winds 〕)〉.
（O'）（関代）（V）（O）

80

訳 ¹太陽は私たちの大気を不均等に温めるので，ある部分が別の部分より温かくなる。²この温かい部分が上昇し，他の空気がそれに取って代わろうと吹き込んでくる。そしてそのことで私たちは風が吹いていると感じるのだ。³私たちは風のエネルギーを，てっぺんに大きなプロペラのついた高い塔を建設することにより利用できる。⁴風が吹いてそのプロペラを回し，プロペラが電気を発生させるように発電機を回転させる。⁵私たちは，「ウィンドファーム（風力発電地帯）」を作ってより多くの電気を発生させるために，このような塔を数多くまとめて建設する傾向がある。⁶塔が多ければ多いほど，風が吹けば吹くほど，プロペラが大きければ大きいほど，より多くの電気を作ることができる。⁷強くて一定の風が吹く場所に風力発電地帯を建設しないと価値はない。

🖊**Check!** 第2文 … and we feel a wind blowing の feel は知覚動詞の用法。feel O *doing* で「O が〜しているのを感じる」の意味。

語句

heat	動	熱する，温める
atmosphere	名	大気
unevenly	副	不均等に，不規則に
warm	形	温かい
rise up	熟	上昇する
blow in	熟	吹き込む
replace	動	取って代わる
propeller	名	プロペラ，推進器
round	副	回って

turn	動	回転させる，回す
generator	名	発電機
produce	動	生産する，生み出す
electricity	名	電気
tend to *do*	熟	〜する傾向がある
It is worth *doing*		
	熟	〜するのは価値がある，〜するだけのことはある
steady	形	一定の，絶え間ない

第3段落 文の構造と語句のチェック

¹The best places 〔 for wind farms 〕 are (in coastal areas), (at the tops 〔 of
　　　S　　　　　　　　　　　　V　①　　　　　　　　　　　　　　②

rounded hills 〕), (on open plains) and (in gaps 〔 in mountains 〕) — places 〔 where
　　　　③　　　　　　　　　　　　等接 ④　　　　　　　　　　　　　　　　　関副

the wind is strong and reliable 〕. ²Some are offshore. ³(To be worthwhile), you
　　S　　V　　C　　等接②　C　　　　S　　V　　C　　　　　　　　　　　　　　S
　　　　　　①

need an average wind speed of around 25 km/h. ⁴Most wind farms 〔 in the UK 〕
　V　　　　　　　　　　O　　　　　　　　　　　　　　　S

are (in Cornwall or Wales). ⁵Isolated places [such as farms] may have
　V　　　　　　　　①　　等接　②　　　　　S　　　　　　　　　　　　　　　V

their own wind generators. ⁶Several wind farms supply electricity (to homes
　　　　O　　　　　　　　　　　S　　　　　　　V　　　O

[around Los Angeles in California]).

訳 ¹風力発電地帯を作るのに最も適した場所は，沿岸地域や丸みを帯びた丘のてっぺん，開けた平原，山の谷間など，風が強くて，確実に吹いてくれる場所だ。²中には沖合にあるものもある。³発電をするに値するためには，およそ時速25キロメートルの平均風速が必要である。⁴イギリスのほとんどの風力発電地帯はコーンウォールまたはウェールズにある。⁵農場のような孤立した場所には，その場所専用の風力発電装置があるかもしれない。⁶いくつかの風力発電地帯がカリフォルニア州ロサンゼルス周辺の家庭に電力を供給している。

語句

coastal	形 沿岸の		**reliable**	形	確かな，あてになる
rounded	形 丸みを帯びた，曲線的な		offshore	副	沖合に
open	形 広々とした，開けた		**worthwhile**	形	価値がある
plain	名 平原，平野		**average**	形	平均の
gap	名 谷間，峡谷，峠		**isolated**	形	孤立した，隔絶した
			supply	動	供給する

第4段落　文の構造と語句のチェック

¹The propellers are large, (to take energy out (from the largest possible
　　S　　　　　　V　　C　　　　V′　　O′

volume of air)). ²The angle of the blades can be changed, (to cope with varying
　　　　　　　　　　　S　　　　　　　　　　V

　　　　　　　　　①　　　　　　　等接 ②
wind speeds), and the generator and propeller can turn (to face the wind)
　　　　　　　等接　　　　S　　　　　　　　　　　　V

(wherever it comes from). ³Some designs use vertical turbines, which don't
　従接　　S　　V　　　　　　　　S　　　　V　　　O　　　　　関代

need to be turned (to face the wind). ⁴The towers are tall, (to get
　V　　　　　　　　　　　　　　　　　　　　　　S　　　V　C　　　V′

the propellers <u>as</u> high <u>as possible</u>, (up to ⟨ <u>where</u> the wind <u>is</u> <u>stronger</u> ⟩)). ⁵This
　　　　　　O′　　　　　　　　　　　　関副　　S　　　V　　C　　　　　S

<u>means</u> ⟨ <u>that</u> the land beneath <u>can still be used</u> (for farming)⟩.
　V　　O従接　　　S　　　　　　　　V

> 【訳】¹可能な限り大きな体積の空気からエネルギーを取り出すために，プロペラは大きくなっている。²ブレードの角度は，変化する風速に対処できるよう，変えられるようになっており，風がどこから吹いてきても，発電機とプロペラはその風の方を向くことができるようになっている。³一部の設計では垂直のタービンが使われており，これは風の方を向くために回転させる必要がない。⁴プロペラを，できるだけ高く，風がより強い場所に届かせるために，塔は高くなっている。⁵このことは，下の土地が依然として農業に利用できることを意味する。

Check! 第3文 Some designs use vertical turbines, which don't need to be turned to face the wind. の which は【非制限用法】の関係代名詞で，vertical turbines が先行詞。

Check! 第4文 …, up to where the wind is stronger. の up to は「～まで，～に達して」の意味の前置詞句。where は関係副詞で，where の直前に先行詞 the place が省略されている。

語句

take out ~	熟	～を取り出す
volume	名	体積，容量
angle	名	角度
blade	名	(プロペラなどの)ブレード，羽根，刃
cope with ~	熟	～に対処する
vary	動	変化する，変動する

face	動	面する，向かう
wherever	接	どこに…しても
vertical	形	垂直の
turbine	名	タービン (＊回転する原動機)
beneath	副	下に，下の方に
farming	名	農業

文法事項の整理 ⑦　the＋比較級

第 2 段落第 6 文の〈the＋比較級〉についてみてみよう。

The more towers, **the more** wind, and **the larger** the propellers, **the more** electricity we can make.

　比較にはさまざまな定型表現がある。ここで，比較級に the がつく表現を整理しておこう。

■**比較級に the がつく定型表現**

① **The＋比較級〜，the＋比較級 …**「〜すればするほど…」

　　例　The older we grow, the poorer our memory becomes.
　　　　「年を取れば取るほど，記憶力が悪くなる」

② **the＋比較級＋of the two**「2 者のうちより…なほう」

　　例　My brother is the taller of the two boys.
　　　　「私の弟は 2 人の少年のうち，より背が高いほうです」

③ **(all) the＋比較級＋理由〜**「〜のせいでよりいっそう…」

　　例　I like him all the better for his faults.
　　　　＝ I like him all the better because he has faults.
　　　　「私は彼に欠点があるからこそ，よりいっそう彼のことが好きだ」

④ **none the＋比較級＋理由〜**「〜であるにもかかわらず…ない」

　　例　I like him none the better for his kindness.
　　　　＝ I like him none the better because he is kind.
　　　　「私は彼が親切であるにもかかわらず，彼のことが好きでない」

⑤ **none the less＋理由〜**「〜であるにもかかわらず…だ」

　　例　I like him none the less for his faults.
　　　　＝ I like him none the less because he has faults.
　　　　「私は彼に欠点があるにもかかわらず，彼のことが好きだ」

■**第 2 段落第 6 文**

The more towers, the more wind, and the larger the propellers, the

84

more electricity we can make.

▶ 〈The＋比較級〜，the＋比較級 ...〉「〜すればするほど…」のパターンだが，前半部分にあたる〈The＋比較級〜〉が A, B, and C の形で３つ並列されている点に注意。また，この構文では SV がなかったり，be 動詞が省略されたりすることも多い。省略を補うと，以下のようになる。

▶ The more towers (there are), the more wind (there is), and the larger the propellers (are), the more electricity we can make.

確認問題

1. 次の和訳と対応する英語の語句を，頭文字を参考にして書き，空欄を完成させよう。

(各１点× 20)

①	i	動	かんがいする，（作物を）うるおす
②	g	動	すりつぶす，粉にする
③	c	名	穀物(小麦，トウモロコシなど)
④	t	名	言葉，用語
⑤	h	動	熱する，温める
⑥	a	名	大気(＝air)
⑦	r	動	取って代わる
⑧	p	動	生産する，生み出す
⑨	e	名	電気
⑩	s	形	一定の，絶え間ない
⑪	c	形	沿岸の
⑫	r	形	確かな，あてになる
⑬	w	形	価値がある
⑭	a	形	平均の
⑮	s	動	供給する
⑯	v	名	体積，容量

⑰	a	名	角度
⑱	v	動	変化する，変動する
⑲	f	動	面する，向かう
⑳	v	形	垂直の

2. 次の[　]内の語句を並べ替えて，意味の通る英文を完成させよう。(各5点×2)

① The wind blows the propeller round, [to / turns / electricity / generator / which / a / produce].

② It's only [wind / in / building / farms / places / worth] that have strong, steady winds.

3. 次の英文を和訳してみよう。(10点)

The more towers, the more wind, and the larger the propellers, the more electricity we can make.

ディクテーションしてみよう！

33・36

今回学習した英文に出てきた語句・表現を，＿＿＿＿に書き取ろう。

33　We've used the wind as an energy source for a long time. The Babylonians and Chinese were using wind power to pump water for ❶＿＿＿＿＿＿＿＿＿＿＿＿＿＿＿＿ 4,000 years ago, and sailing boats were around long before that. Wind power was used in the Middle Ages, in Europe, to grind corn, ❷＿＿＿＿＿＿＿＿＿＿＿＿＿＿ the term "windmill" comes from.

34　The sun heats our atmosphere unevenly, so some parts become warmer than others. These warm parts rise up, other air blows in to replace them — and we ❸＿＿＿＿＿＿＿＿＿＿＿＿＿＿＿＿＿＿＿. We can use the energy in the wind by building a tall tower, with a large propeller on the top. The wind blows the propeller round, which turns a generator to produce electricity. We tend to build many of these towers together, to make a "wind farm" and produce more electricity. The more towers, the more wind, and the larger the propellers, the more electricity we can make. It's only ❹_____ wind farms in places that have strong, steady winds.

35 The best places for wind farms are in coastal areas, at the tops of rounded hills, ❺_____ and in gaps in mountains — places where the wind is strong and reliable. Some are offshore. To be worthwhile, you need ❻_____ of around 25 km/h. Most wind farms in the UK are in Cornwall or Wales. Isolated places such as farms may have their own wind generators. Several wind farms supply electricity to homes around Los Angeles in California.

36 The propellers are large, to ❼_____ from the largest possible volume of air. The angle of the blades can be changed, to cope with varying wind speeds, and the generator and propeller can turn to face the wind ❽_____ it comes from. Some designs use ❾_____ turbines, which don't need to be turned to face the wind. The towers are tall, to get the propellers as high as possible, ❿_____ _____ the wind is stronger. This means that the land beneath can still be used for farming.

確認問題の答 1. ① irrigate ② grind ③ corn ④ term ⑤ heat
⑥ atmosphere ⑦ replace ⑧ produce ⑨ electricity ⑩ steady
⑪ coastal ⑫ reliable ⑬ worthwhile ⑭ average ⑮ supply ⑯ volume
⑰ angle ⑱ vary ⑲ face ⑳ vertical

2. ① which turns a generator to produce electricity（第2段落 第4文）
② worth building wind farms in places（第2段落 最終文）

3. 塔が多ければ多いほど，風が吹けば吹くほど，プロペラが大きければ大きいほど，より多くの電気を作ることができる。（第2段落 第6文）

ディクテーションしてみよう！の答 ❶ irrigating crops ❷ which is where
❸ feel a wind blowing ❹ worth building ❺ on open plains
❻ an average wind speed ❼ take energy out ❽ wherever ❾ vertical
❿ up to where

アドバイス ❹ worth の /θ/ が聞き取れるかどうかがポイント。worse の /s/ と音で区別できるようにしよう。
❻ an の /n/ の音と後ろの average の /æ/ の音がつながり「ナ」のように聞こえる（⇒連結）。

解答

問1	1年半もたたないうちに，フィリスは英語が流ちょうになっており，（それ以前から）ラテン語も学び始めていた。

問2	Phillis Wheatley

問3	**（ア）** born	**（ウ）** taught	**（オ）** assigned	**（カ）** Treated

問4	**（イ）** ②	**（ク）** ①	**（ケ）** ①	**（コ）** ②	**（サ）** ②

問5	① ×	② ×	③ ○	④ ×	⑤ ×	⑥ ×	⑦ ○

解説

問1 以下のポイントをおさえよう！

☑ within は前置詞で「～以内に，～もたたないうちに」の意味。

☑ a year and a half は「1年半」。

☑ had also begun は過去完了形なので，1年半が経過するまでに，すでにラテン語を学び始めていたことになる。

問2

下線部の意味は「非常に並外れた女性の奴隷」。extraordinary は「並外れた，ずば抜けた」の意味。第1段落第1，2文から，フィリス・ウィートリーが女性の奴隷であったことがわかる。また，第1段落後半と第2段落前半から，フィリス・ウィートリーが詩を作ることで有名になったこともわかる。

問3

（ア） be born で「生まれる」の意味。bear「生む」の活用は **bear-bore-born [borne]**。【受動】を表す過去分詞の borne は，直後に by ～（生んだ人）が続く場合のみ用いる。

> **例** He is the only child **borne** by the lady.
> 「彼はその女性が生んだ唯一の子だ」

（ウ） When から始まる副詞節が終わった後なので，**（ウ）**を含む文は主節である。副詞節の動詞が saw なので，ここも過去形が適切。teach の活用は

teach-taught-taught。

(**オ**) assign は「割り当てる，課す」の意味。ここでは her と名詞 role「役割」
の間なので，「彼女の課された役割」と考えて，【受動】を表す過去分詞
にする。

(**カ**) treat *A* as *B* で「**A を B として扱う**」。A にあたる目的語がないこと，
また後ろに by があることに注目し，受動態を表す過去分詞にする。こ
こでは直前に Being が省略された分詞構文(【付帯状況】を表すと考えて
よい)となっている。

問4

(**イ**) 直前に，奴隷船でアメリカに来てボストンで買われたとの内容があるの
で，servant「召使い」が適切。

(**ク**) 空所の前に returned to「～へ戻ってきた」とあるので，イングランドに
旅行する前にどこにいたのかを考える。第1段落第2文参照。

(**ケ**) 第2段落後半にはイングランドの宮廷に招かれたこと，第3段落にはベ
ンジャミン・フランクリンやジョージ・ワシントンの目にとまったこと
が書かれているので，国際的な「名声」を得たと考える。選択肢の意味
は，①「名声」，②「自由」，③「旅行」。achieve fame で「名声を得る」。

(**コ**) 奴隷であったフィリスが解放されたとの記述が第2段落最終文にあるが，
最終段落第2文には解放後も主人のもとで暮らしたとあるので，解放さ
れたことを特に喜んでいないとするのが文脈に合う。選択肢の意味は，
①「活動」，②「解放」，③「奴隷制」。

(**サ**) the beloved (　　) of となっているので，空所には名詞が入る。よって，
①は不可(liberate は「～を解放する」の意味の動詞)。また，than の前
の as a free black woman との対比を考えると，③も不自然。

問5

① 「フィリスは17世紀なかばにアメリカに来た」
▶ 第1段落第2文と不一致。1761年は18世紀。
② 「ウィートリー夫妻には子供がおらず，フィリスを我が娘と思っていた」
▶ 第1段落第3文と不一致。ウィートリー夫妻には娘がいたことがわかる。
③ 「フィリスはアメリカに来たとき，英語が得意ではなかった」

▶ 第1段落第3文に，ウィートリー夫妻の娘が(英語の)読み方を教えたとの記述があるので，当初は英語が不得手であったと判断できる。

④「フィリスはニューイングランドの新聞社で働いた」

▶ 第1段落第6文と不一致。作品が新聞に掲載されたのであって，新聞社に勤務したわけではない。本文の work は「著作，作品」の意味。

⑤「フィリスはいい召使いだったのだが，ウィートリー一家は彼女をあまり気に入っていなかった」

▶ 第2段落第1文に娘のように扱われたこと，第4段落第2文に beloved「愛された」とあることと矛盾する。

⑥「ウィートリー夫人は死の間際にフィリスを解放した」

▶ 第2段落最終文によれば，フィリスを解放したのは夫のジョン・ウィートリーである。

⑦ **「アメリカの独立を求めて戦った黒人もいた」**

▶ 第3段落最後の2文と一致。

▼

それでは次に，段落ごとに詳しくみていこう。

37

第1段落　文の構造と語句のチェック

¹Phillis Wheatley was born (in Senegal). ²She arrived (in America) (on a
　　S　　　　　　　V　　　　　　　　　　S　　　V
slave ship) (around 1761), when she was seven or eight years old, and was
　　　　　　　　　　　　　　関副　S　V　　　　　　　C　　　　　等接
purchased (in Boston) (by John Wheatley), who wanted a personal servant
　V　　　　　　　　　　　　　　　　　　　　関代　V　　　O
[for his wife, Susanna Wheatley]. ³(When the Wheatleys' daughter saw Phillis
　　　└─同格─┘　　　　　　従接　　　　　　S　　　　　V　O
[trying to write the alphabet (with chalk) (on the wall)]), she taught her to
　C　V'　　　　O'　　　　　　　　　　　　　　　　　　　　S　　V　　O

90

read. ⁴(Within a year and a half), Phillis was fluent (in English) and had
   O   S   V①   C   等接

also begun to study Latin. ⁵(By the time she was thirteen) she was writing
   V②   O   従接   S   V   C   S   V

poetry. ⁶Her work began to appear (in New England newspapers), and she
 O   S   V   等接 S

became a regional celebrity. ⁷She had found a way 〔 out of the normal
 V   C   S   V   O

restrictions 〔 of her assigned role 〔 in life 〕〕〕(through poetry).

訳 ¹フィリス・ウィートリーはセネガルで生まれた。²彼女は 1761 年頃に奴隷船でアメリカに到着し，7 歳か 8 歳でボストンでジョン・ウィートリーに買われた。彼は妻のスザンナ・ウィートリーのための個人的な召使いを求めていたのだった。³ウィートリー夫妻の娘は，フィリスが壁にチョークでアルファベットを書こうとしているのを見かけたとき，フィリスに読み方を教えた。⁴1 年半もたたないうちに，フィリスは英語が流ちょうになっており，（それ以前から）ラテン語も学び始めていた。⁵13 歳になるまでには詩を書いていた。⁶彼女の作品はニューイングランドの新聞に掲載されるようになり，彼女は地域の有名人になった。⁷彼女は詩を通じて，人生において課された役割の通常の制約から脱する道を見つけたのだ。

語句

bear	動 生む	**fluent**	形 流ちょうな
＊活用：bear-bore-born [borne]		**Latin**	名 ラテン語
slave	名 奴隷	**by the time ...**	熟 …するときまでに
purchase	動 買う，購入する	**poetry**	名 詩，詩歌
personal	形 個人の，私的な	**work**	名 著作，作品
servant	名 使用人，召使い	**appear**	動 載る，掲載される
daughter	名 娘	**regional**	形 地域の，地方の
try to *do*	熟 ～しようとする	**celebrity**	名 有名人
alphabet	名 アルファベット	**normal**	形 普通の
chalk	名 チョーク	**restriction**	名 制限，制約
within	前 ～以内に，～もたたないうちに	**assign**	動 割り当てる，課す
		role	名 役割

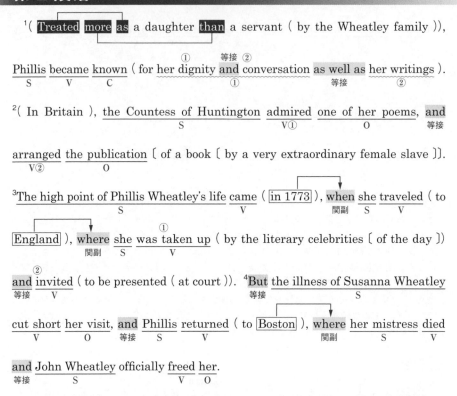

¹(Treated more as a daughter than a servant (by the Wheatley family)),

Phillis became known (for her dignity and conversation as well as her writings).
　S　　V　　C　　　　　　　　①　　　　　等接　　　　　等接　　　　②

②(In Britain), the Countess of Huntington admired one of her poems, and
　　　　　　　　　　　S　　　　　　　　　　V①　　　　　O　　　　等接

arranged the publication [of a book [by a very extraordinary female slave]].
　V②　　　　O

³The high point of Phillis Wheatley's life came (in 1773), when she traveled (to
　　　　　　S　　　　　　　　　　　V　　　　　　　　関副　S　　V

England), where she was taken up (by the literary celebrities [of the day])
　　　　　関副　S　　　V

and invited (to be presented (at court)). ⁴But the illness of Susanna Wheatley
等接　V　　　　　　　　　　　　　　　　　等接　　S

cut short her visit, and Phillis returned (to Boston), where her mistress died
　V　　O　　等接　S　　V　　　　　　　　　関副　S　　V

and John Wheatley officially freed her.
等接　S　　　　　　　V　　O

訳 ¹ウィートリー家からは召使いというよりむしろ娘として扱われ，フィリスは著作物だけでなく気品の高さや交友でも知られるようになった。²イギリスではハンティントン伯爵夫人が彼女の詩の1つを賞賛し，非常に並外れた女性の奴隷による本の出版を手配した。³フィリス・ウィートリーの人生の頂点は1773年にめぐってきた。その年，彼女はイングランドへと旅行し，そこで当時の文学界の著名人たちに支援され，宮廷で正式に紹介を受けるよう招かれた。⁴しかし，スザンナ・ウィートリーが病気になったため，彼女のイングランド訪問は早めに切り上げられ，フィリスはボストンに戻った。ボストンでは彼女の女主人が亡くなり，ジョン・ウィートリーは正式に彼女を自由の身にした。

語句

treat *A* as *B*	熟 AをBとして扱う	conversation	名 交際，社交
more *A* than *B*	熟 BというよりむしろA	*A* as well as *B*	熟 BだけでなくAも
dignity	名 品位，気品	writing	名 著作，（書いた）作品
		countess	名 伯爵夫人

92

admire	動	賞賛する	**invite**	動	招待する，招く
poem	名	詩	present	動	（正式に）紹介する，引き合わ
arrange	動	手配する，準備する			せる
publication	名	出版	**court**	名	宮廷，王宮
extraordinary	形	並外れた，ずば抜けた	cut short ～	熟	～を切り上げる，早めに終える
female	形	女性の	mistress	名	（女性の）主人，所有者
take up ～	熟	～を支援する，援助する	**officially**	副	正式に，公式に
literary	形	文学の	**free**	動	解放する，自由にする
of the day	熟	当時の，その時代の			

第3段落　文の構造と語句のチェック

¹She was the first American writer〔to achieve international fame〕.
S　V　　　　　　　C

²Benjamin Franklin read her work, which sometimes compared the experience of
S　　　　　　V　　O　　　関代　　　　　　　V　　　　　　O

a slave（to that〔of American colonists〔under British tyranny〕〕）. ³George
＝
the experience

Washington invited her（to visit him（at his camp）（during the War of
S　　　　V　　O

Independence〕〕. ⁴Some historians credit her（with Washington's decision〔to
S　　　　　V　O

allow black men to serve in his army〕〕.
V′　O′　　　　C′

訳 ¹彼女は国際的な名声を獲得した最初のアメリカ人作家であった。²ベンジャミン・フランクリンは彼女の作品を読んだが，その作品は時に奴隷の経験をイギリスの圧政下におけるアメリカ人開拓者の経験にたとえるものであった。³ジョージ・ワシントンは独立戦争中，彼女を野営地の彼のもとに来るよう招いた。⁴歴史家の中には，ワシントンが黒人の従軍を許可する決断をしたのは彼女の功績であると考える者もいる。

語句
achieve	動	成し遂げる，（名声を）獲得する	**compare A to B**	熟	A を B にたとえる
international	形	国際的な	**experience**	名	経験
fame	名	名声	colonist	名	（植民地）開拓者，入植者
			tyranny	名	暴政，圧政

93

camp	名 野営地	decision	名	決意，決断
the War of Independence		allow	動	許可する
	名 (アメリカ)独立戦争	serve	動	仕える，奉仕する
historian 名 歴史家		army	名	軍隊
credit A with B 熟 A(人)に B の功績があると考える				

第4段落 文の構造と語句のチェック

¹Phillis Wheatley found no happiness (in her own liberty). ²She continued to
　　　　S　　　　　V　　　O　　　　　　　　　　　　　　　　　　S　　　　　V

live (with her old master) (until his death), but the people of Boston had
　　　　　　　　　　　　　　　　　　　　　　　等接　　　　S　　　　　　V

much less interest (in her) (as a free black woman) than they did (when she
　　　　O　　　　　　　　　　　　　　　　　　　　　　　S　V　　従接　S

was the beloved slave [of a prominent white family]).
V　　　　C

> 訳 ¹フィリス・ウィートリーは自らの解放をうれしく思うことはなかった。²彼女は元の主人が死ぬまで彼とともに暮らし続けた。しかし，ボストンの人々は解放された黒人女性としてよりむしろ，有名な白人家庭の愛される奴隷であったときに，はるかに高い関心を彼女に対して示した。

語句

happiness	名 幸福，喜び	master	名	(男性の)主人
liberty	名 自由，解放	death	名	死
continue to do	熟 ～し続ける	beloved	形	愛される
		prominent	形	有名な

文法事項の整理 ⑧ 関係詞の非制限用法

第 1 段落第 2 文の when についてみてみよう。

She arrived in America on a slave ship around 1761, **when** she was seven or eight years old, ...

■関係代名詞の非制限用法

「制限用法」の関係代名詞は前の名詞（先行詞）を修飾（後ろから訳す）。

例 He has two brothers <u>who</u> work in this office.
「彼にはこの会社で働いている 2 人の兄弟がいる」

これに対し，**「非制限用法」**の関係代名詞は，〈, (コンマ)＋関係代名詞〉の形で，先行詞について補足説明をする。和訳するときは，前から訳す。

例 He has two brothers, <u>who</u> work in this office.
「彼には 2 人の兄弟がいて，その 2 人はこの会社で働いている」

＊訳し方は，文脈に応じ，「〜，そして…」「〜，しかし…」「〜，だから…」「〜，なぜなら…」などとする。

〈, (コンマ)＋which〉は主節（の一部）を指すことができる。

例 I tried to read the book, <u>which</u> was written in easy English.
「私はその本を読もうとした。それは易しい英語で書かれていたからだ」
▶ which は the book を指す。

例 I tried to read the book, <u>which</u> I found impossible.
「私はその本を読もうとしたが，それが無理だとわかった」
▶ which は to read the book を指す。

例 I tried to read the book, <u>which</u> surprised our teacher.
「私はその本を読もうとしたが，そのことで先生はびっくりした」
▶ which は I tried to read the book という主節全体を指す。

■関係副詞の非制限用法

「制限用法」の関係副詞も前の名詞（先行詞）を修飾（後ろから訳す）。

例 Tokyo is one of the cities <u>where</u> I want to live some day.
「東京はいつか住んでみたい都市の 1 つだ」

これに対し，**「非制限用法」**の関係副詞は〈**, (コンマ)＋関係副詞**〉の形で，先行詞について補足説明をする。和訳するときは，前から訳す。なお，この用法を持つ関係副詞は **when** と **where** のみである。

例 I want to visit Kyoto, <u>where</u> there are many old temples and shrines.
「私は京都に行ってみたい。そこには多くの古い寺や神社があるからだ」

■第 1 段落第 2 文

... around 1761, when she was seven or eight years old, and was purchased in Boston by John Wheatley, who wanted ....

▶ when は関係副詞の非制限用法で around 1761 についての補足説明。who は関係代名詞の非制限用法で，John Wheatley についての補足説明。なお，先行詞が固有名詞の場合，必ず非制限用法になる。

■第 2 段落第 3 文

The high point of Phillis Wheatley's life came in 1773, when she traveled to England, where she was taken up ....

▶ when は関係副詞の非制限用法で in 1773 についての補足説明。where も関係副詞の非制限用法で，England についての補足説明。

■第 2 段落第 4 文

... Phillis returned to Boston, where her mistress died and John Wheatley officially freed her.

▶ where は関係副詞の非制限用法で Boston についての補足説明。

■第 3 段落第 2 文

Benjamin Franklin read her work, which sometimes compared the experience of a slave to that of American colonists under British tyranny.

▶ which は関係代名詞の非制限用法で，her work についての補足説明。

確認問題

40点

1. 次の和訳と対応する英語の語句を，頭文字を参考にして書き，空欄を完成させよう。

(各1点×20)

①	s		名	奴隷
②	p		動	買う，購入する
③	f		形	流ちょうな
④	r		形	地域の，地方の
⑤	r		名	制限，制約
⑥	t	*A* a *B*	熟	AをBとして扱う
⑦	d		名	品位，気品
⑧	a		動	賞賛する
⑨	p		名	出版
⑩	e		形	並外れた，ずば抜けた
⑪	l		形	文学の
⑫	o		副	正式に，公式に
⑬	a		動	成し遂げる，（名声を）獲得する
⑭	f		名	名声
⑮	c	*A* t *B*	熟	AをBにたとえる
⑯	t		名	暴政，圧政
⑰	s		動	仕える，奉仕する
⑱	a		名	軍隊
⑲	l		名	自由，解放
⑳	p		形	有名な

2. 次の[ ]内の語句を並べ替えて，意味の通る英文を完成させよう。(各5点×2)

① Treated more [than / a / daughter / as] a servant by the Wheatley family, Phillis became known for her dignity and conversation as well as her writings.

② Benjamin Franklin read her work, which sometimes [the experience / compared / of / that / a slave / to] of American colonists under British tyranny.

3. 次の英文を和訳してみよう。(10 点)

Some historians credit her with Washington's decision to allow black men to serve in his army.

ディクテーションしてみよう！

今回学習した英文に出てきた語句・表現を，＿＿＿＿に書き取ろう。

38 Phillis Wheatley was born in Senegal. She arrived in America ❶__ _____ around 1761, when she was seven or eight years old, and was purchased in Boston by John Wheatley, who wanted a personal servant for his wife, Susanna Wheatley. When the Wheatleys' daughter saw Phillis trying to write the alphabet with chalk on the wall, she taught her to read. ❷_____, Phillis was fluent in English and had also begun to study Latin. By the time she was thirteen she was writing poetry. Her work began to appear in New England newspapers, and she became a regional celebrity. She had found a way out of the normal restrictions of her ❸_____ in life through poetry.

39 ❹_____ a daughter than a servant by the Wheatley family, Phillis became known for her dignity and conversation as well as her writings. In Britain, the Countess of Huntington admired one of her poems, and arranged the publication of a book by a very extraordinary female slave. The high point of Phillis Wheatley's life came in 1773, when she traveled to England, where she was ❺_____ by the literary celebrities of the day and invited to be presented at court. But the illness of

Susanna Wheatley ❻_____, and Phillis returned to Boston, where her mistress died and John Wheatley officially freed her.

40 She was the first American writer to achieve international fame. Benjamin Franklin ❼_____, which sometimes compared the experience of a slave to that of American colonists under British tyranny. George Washington invited her to visit him at his camp during the War of Independence. Some historians ❽_____ _____ Washington's decision to allow black men to serve in his army.

41 Phillis Wheatley found no happiness ❾_____ _____. She continued to live with her old master until his death, but the people of Boston had much less interest in her as a free black woman than they did when she was the beloved slave of a ❿_____ _____ family.

確認問題の答 1. ① slave ② purchase ③ fluent ④ regional ⑤ restriction ⑥ treat, as ⑦ dignity ⑧ admire ⑨ publication ⑩ extraordinary ⑪ literary ⑫ officially ⑬ achieve ⑭ fame ⑮ compare, to ⑯ tyranny ⑰ serve ⑱ army ⑲ liberty ⑳ prominent

2. ① as a daughter than （第2段落　第1文）
② compared the experience of a slave to that （第3段落　第2文）

3. 歴史家の中には，ワシントンが黒人の従軍を許可する決断をしたのは彼女の功績であると考える者もいる。
（第3段落　最終文）

ディクテーションしてみよう！の答 ❶ on a slave ship ❷ Within a year and a half ❸ assigned role ❹ Treated more as ❺ taken up ❻ cut short her visit ❼ read her work ❽ credit her with ❾ in her own liberty ❿ prominent white

アドバイス ❼代名詞，前置詞，接続詞，冠詞などの機能語は，強形・弱形という2種類の発音を持ち，原則として弱形で，例外的に文中で重要な意味を持つ場合は強形で発音される。her の弱形は /ər/，強形は /hə́:r/ であり，ここでは弱形。つまり，/h/ の音がほぼ発音されず，冠詞の a に近い音になる。

解答

問1	(ア) ③	(イ) ①	(ウ) ②	(エ) ②	(オ) ④
	(カ) ③	(キ) ④	(ク) ①	(ケ) ②	(コ) ③

問2	②, ⑤, ⑨

解 説

問1

(ア)「とても楽に」 選択肢はそれぞれ，①「とても頻繁に」，②「とても苦労して」，③「とても容易に」，④「ほとんど理由もなく」の意味。

(イ)「～に参加する」 選択肢はそれぞれ，①「～において役割を果たす」，②「創造する」，③「～でうまくやる」，④「教える」の意味。

(ウ)「～を奪われて」 選択肢はそれぞれ，①「～に加えられて」，②「～との接触を与えられずに」，③「～につながって」，④「～から盗まれて」。②の deny は，第3文型($S+V+O$)で「O を否定する」，第4文型($S+V+O_1+O_2$)で「O_1 に O_2 を与えない」の意味。

(エ)「著しく」 選択肢はそれぞれ，①「たいてい」，②「とても」，③「ある程度は」，④「まったく～ない」の意味。

(オ)「苦労して」 選択肢はそれぞれ，①「長い間」，②「無邪気に」，③「さまざまな方法で」，④「おおいに苦労しながら」の意味。

(カ)「…する限り」 選択肢はそれぞれ，①「…する間に」，②「…と同様に」，③「もし…ならば，…という条件で」，④「同様に」。as long as … は「…する限り」の意味だが，while に近い意味で**【時間】**を表す場合(例 as long as I live「生きている限り」)と，**【条件】**を表す場合(例 as long as you keep quiet「静かにしている限り」)の2つの意味がある。本文では後者の意味。

(キ)「～に触れさせられて」 選択肢はそれぞれ，①「示す」，②「買われる」，③「習得する」，④「～と接触する」。expose *A* to *B* は「A(人)を B(考え方，文化など)に触れさせる，さらす」の意味。ここはその受け身。

（ク）「上手な，熟達した」　選択肢はそれぞれ，①「巧みな，熟練した」，②「現実的な」，③「おもしろい，愉快な」，④「幸運な」の意味。

（ケ）「影響されて」　選択肢はそれぞれ，①「改良されて」，②「影響されて」，③「示されて」，④「理解されて」の意味。

（コ）「重大な，決定的な」　選択肢はそれぞれ，①「大きな」，②「開放的な」，③「重要な」，④「浅い」の意味。

問2

① 「コミュニケーションをするために言語を習得する機会を逃す子供は決していない」

▶ 第1段落第2文と不一致。miss out on ～ は「～の機会を逃す」の意味。

② **「言語は我々を人間らしくする主たる要素の1つである」**

▶ 第1段落第1文の and plays 以降と一致。

③ 「子供たちはいかなる年齢でも問題なく言語学習を始めることができる」

▶ 第1段落最終文，第2段落最終文，第3段落第5，6文と不一致。

④ 「大変な努力の後，ヴィクトールは少々の言葉を話せるようになった」

▶ 第2段落最終文と不一致。

⑤ **「イタールはヴィクトールに少し読むことを教えるのには成功したが，話すことを教えるのには成功しなかった」**

▶ 第2段落最終文と一致。

⑥ 「耳の聞こえない子供たちは，言語から隔離された子供たちよりも状況が悪い」

▶ 最終段落第1文と不一致。be worse off（than ～）で「（～よりも）状況がひどい，暮らし向きが悪い」の意味。

⑦ 「耳の聞こえない子供や言語から隔離された子供にとっては，語彙よりも文法を習得する方が容易である」

▶ 最終段落最後の2文と不一致。

⑧ 「手話は耳の聞こえない子供たちにとって無益である」

▶ 最終段落第2文と不一致。

⑨ **「比較的早い年齢までに文法を習得することが不可欠である」**

▶ 最終段落最終文と一致。

第1段落　文の構造と語句のチェック

Growing up without language

¹It is almost impossible 〈 **for** us **to** imagine growing up without language 〉,
仮S V　　　　　　　 C　　　 真S S′　 V′

which develops (in our minds) (so effortlessly) (in early childhood) and plays
関代　 V①　　　　　　　　　　　　　　　　　　　　　　　　　　　 等接　 V②

such a central role (in 〈 **defining** us **as** human 〉 and 〈 allowing us to participate
O　　　　　　 ①　　　　　　　　 等接　 ②　 V′　 O′　　 C′

in our culture 〉). ²Nevertheless, 〈 being **deprived of** language 〉 occasionally
　　　　　　　　　　　　　　　　　　　 S

happens. ³(In recent centuries) children have been found living in the wild,
V　　　　　　　　　　　　　　　 S　　 V　　　　　　 C

　┌── being 省略
(said to have been raised by wolves or other animals and **deprived of** human
　　　　　　　　　 ①　　　　　　　　　　　　 等接　　　　　 ②

contact.) ⁴It is hard 〈 to know the real stories 〔 behind these cases 〕〉, but they
　　　　　 仮S V C 真S V′　　　 O′　　　　　　　　　　 等接　 S

are all strikingly similar (with respect to language). ⁵The pattern is 〈 that
V　　　 C　　　　　　　　　　　　　　　　　　　　　 S　　 V C 従接
　　 the children
only **those** 〔 rescued early in childhood 〕 developed an ability 〔 to speak 〕〉.
S　　　　　　　　　　　　　　　　 V　　　 O
The children
‖
⁶**Those** 〔 found (**after** they were about nine years old)〕 learned only a few
S　　　　　 従接　 S　 V　　　 C　　　　　　 V①　　　 O

words, or failed to learn language (at all).
　　 等接　 V②　　　 O

訳 　　　　　　　　　　言語なしで成長すること

　¹私たちが言語なしで育つことを想像するのはほとんど不可能である。なぜなら言語は、子供時代の初期にとても容易に頭の中で発達するものであるし、私たちを人間と定義する上で、また、私たちが自分たちの文化に参加することを可能にする上で、とても重要な役割を果たしているからだ。²にもかかわらず、言語を奪われるということが時折起こる。³ここ数百年の間に子供たちが野生の状態で生活しているのが発見され、オオカミやその他の動物によって育てられて人間との接触を奪われたと言われている。⁴このような事例の背後にある真相を知ることは困難だが、言語に関してはみな著しく似通っている。⁵そのパターンとは、幼少期の初期に救われた子供しか言語を話す能力は発達しなかったことだ。⁶およそ9歳以降に発見された子供たちは、ごくわずかの言葉しか覚えなかったか、言語を身につけることがまったくできなかった。

Check! 第1文 ... and allowing us to participate in our culture の〈allow＋O＋to *do*〉は、①「Oが〜するのを許可する」（＝permit）、②「Oが〜するのを可能にする」（＝enable）の2つの意味を持つ。原則として、①はSが人間の場合、②はSが物事の場合である。ここでは②の意味。

Check! 第3文 In recent centuries children have been found living in the wild, said to have been raised by wolves or other animals and deprived of human contact. の said は過去分詞で、前に being が省略された分詞構文（**【付帯状況】**の意味）と考える。have been の後は raised と deprived が並列されている。

語句

imagine	動 想像する		**recent**	形 最近の
develop	動 発達する［させる］		**century**	名 世紀、百年
effortlessly	副 苦労せず、楽に		in the wild	熟 野生で、自然界で
childhood	名 子供時代、幼少期		**raise**	動 育てる
play a role	熟 役割を果たす		wolf	名 オオカミ
central	形 中心的な、主要な			（複数形 wolves）
define *A* as *B*	熟 A を B と定義する		**contact**	名 接触
human	形 人間の		**case**	名 事例、実例
allow	動 可能にする		**strikingly**	副 著しく
participate in ～	熟 〜に参加する		**similar**	形 よく似て、類似して
culture	名 文化		**with respect to ～**	熟 〜に関して
nevertheless	副 にもかかわらず、それなのに		pattern	名 パターン、決まった型
			rescue	動 救う、救助する
deprive *A* of *B*	熟 A から B を奪う		**ability**	名 能力
occasionally	副 時折、時々		**fail to *do***	熟 〜できない、〜しない
			at all	熟 （否定文で）まったく、全然

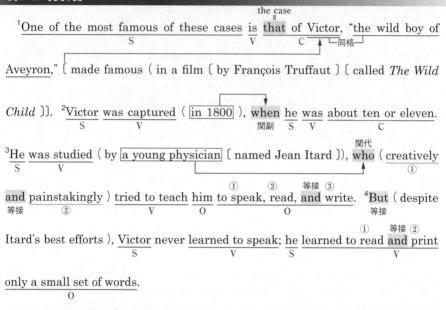

famous	形	有名な		**painstakingly**	副	苦労して，丹念に
wild	形	野生の		**try to** *do*	熟	～しようとする，～しようと努める
capture	動	捕まえる		**despite**	前	～にもかかわらず
study	動	研究する		**effort**	名	努力
physician	名	医師，内科医		**learn to** *do*	熟	～できるようになる
creatively	副	創造的に，独創的に		**print**	動	(活字体で)書く
				a set of ～	熟	一連の～

第3段落　文の構造と語句のチェック

as children without language(like Victor) 省略

¹Children〔without hearing〕are not as handicapped. ²A deaf child can still
　S　　　　　　　　　　　　　　　V　　　C　　　　　　　　　　　　　　S

have language and relate normally (to others) (through signing) — (as long as
V①　　O　等接　V②　　　　　　　　　　　　　　　　　　　　　　　　　　　従接

language development starts early). ³There are a number of studies〔that
　　　　S　　　　　　　V　　　　　　　　　　　V　　　　S　　　　　　　関代

show〈that (the sooner a deaf child is exposed (to a natural sign language),
V　 O 従接　　　　　　　S　　　　V　　 to

〔such as American Sign Language 〕), the more proficient a signer he or she
　　　　　　　　　　　　　　　　　　　　　　C　　　　　　　S

will become 〉〕. ⁴(As in other cases of linguistic isolation), the ability〔of deaf
　V　　　　　　　　従接　　　　　　　　　　　　　　　　　　　　　S

people 〕〔to learn new *words* 〕is not affected (by the age 〔at which they
　　　　　　　　　　　　　　　　　　V　　　　　　　　　　　　　関代　　S

are exposed (to language)〕)). ⁵But their ability 〔to learn grammar 〕is
　V　　　　 to　　　　　　　　　 等接　　S

dramatically affected. ⁶Studies〔of deaf children〔exposed to sign language
　　　　　V　　　　　　　S

(after the preschool years)〕〕show〈that there is a critical period 〔for
　　　　　　　　　　　　　　　　V　 O 従接　　　V　　S

grammatical development 〕, which ends, perhaps, (in the early school-age
　　　　　　　　　　　　　　関代　　V

years)〉.

訳 ¹聴覚を持たない子供たちは，それに比べると不利ではない。²耳の聞こえない子供は，それでも言語を持ち，手話を通じて他者との関係を正常に結ぶことができる——言語の発達が早期に始まっている限りは。³耳の聞こえない子供が，アメリカ手話のような自然な手話に早く触れれば触れるほど，上手に手話を使えるようになる，ということを示す多数の研究がある。⁴言語的隔離の他の事例と同様に，耳の聞こえない人々が新しい言葉を覚える能力は言語に触れる年齢によっては影響されない。⁵しかし，文法を覚える能力は劇的に影響を受ける。⁶就学前の幼児期を過ぎてから手話に触れた，耳の聞こえない子供たちに関する研究が示すところによれば，文法的発達には臨界期が存在し，文法力の発達はおそらく，就学年齢に達してからの数年で終わってしまうというのだ。

Check! 第 1 文 Children without hearing are not as handicapped. では，〈not as [so]＋原級＋as ～〉「～ほど…ない」の後ろの as ～ が省略されている。省略を補うなら，as children without language（like Victor）となろう。

Check! 第 3 文 There are a number of studies that show that the sooner a deaf child is exposed to a natural sign language, such as American Sign Language, the more proficient a signer he or she will become. では，〈The＋比較級～, the＋比較級 ...〉「～すればするほど…」がポイント（→ p. 84 参照）。

語 句

hearing	名	聴力，聴覚
handicapped	形	障害のある，不利な立場にある
deaf	形	耳が聞こえない
relate to ～	熟	～（人）と良い関係を結ぶ，うまく付き合う
normally	副	普通に，正常に
sign	動	手話を用いる
as long as ...	熟	…する限り
development	名	発達
a number of ～	熟	多数の～
study	名	研究，調査
expose A to B	熟	A を B に触れさせる，さらす
natural	形	自然な

sign language	名	手話
such as ～	熟	～のような
proficient	形	上手な，熟達した
signer	名	手話を使う人，手話通訳者
linguistic	形	言語（学）の
isolation	名	孤立，分断，隔離
affect	動	影響する
grammar	名	文法
dramatically	副	劇的に
preschool	形	就学前の
critical	形	重大な，決定的な
▶ **critical period**	名	臨界期
		（＊発達過程において，その時期を過ぎるとある行動の学習が成立しなくなる限界の時期）
grammatical	形	文法の，文法的な
school-age	形	就学年齢の

106

文法事項の整理 ⑨ 「…する限り」

第3段落第2文の as long as についてみてみよう。

... **as long as** language development starts early.

■「…する限り」の意味をもつ接続詞

「…する限り」の意味を表す接続詞には，以下の2つがある。

> 1) **as [so] far as ...**　▶【範囲】を表す。
>
> 2) **as [so] long as ...**　▶【時間】【条件】を表す。
>
> 　　　　　　　　　　　※【時間】の場合，so long as ... は不可。

　このうち，2) の【時間】は while に，【条件】は if only に意味が近い。したがって，while や if only に置き換えられる場合は as [so] long as ...，どちらとも置き換えられない場合は as [so] far as ... と考えるとよい。

① 例　I won't let him have his own way as long as I live.
「私が生きている限り（＝生きている間），彼に好き勝手なことはさせない」
▶ while に近い。【時間】を表す。so long as ... は不可。

② 例　As far as I am concerned, I have no objection to the idea.
「私に関する限り，その見解に対する反論はない」
▶ while や if only とは置き換えられない。【範囲】を表す。as [so] far as S is concerned「S に関する限り」は決まり文句。

③ 例　You can stay in this room, as long as you keep quiet.
「君は静かにしている限り，この部屋にいてよろしい」
▶ if only に近い。【条件】を表す。

④ 例　As far as the eye could reach, nothing was to be seen but snow.
「目が届く限り（＝目が届く範囲内では），雪以外に何も見えなかった」
▶【範囲】を表す。

⑤ 例　As far as I know, he is an honest man.
「私の知る限り（＝私が知っている範囲内では），彼は正直者だ」

▶【範囲】を表す。as [so] far as S know「S が知る限り」(= to the best of S's knowledge) も決まり文句として覚えよう。

⑥ 例 Anything will do as long as it is interesting.
「興味深いものである限り，何でもかまわない」

▶ if only に近い。【条件】を表す。

確認問題

1. 次の和訳と対応する英語の語句を，頭文字を参考にして書き，空欄を完成させよう。 /40点

(各1点 × 20)

① i ＿＿＿＿＿＿ 動 想像する

② d ＿＿＿＿＿＿ 動 発達する［させる］

③ c ＿＿＿＿＿＿ 名 子供時代，幼少期

④ d ＿＿＿ *A* a ＿＿＿ *B* 熟 A を B と定義する

⑤ d ＿＿＿ *A* o ＿ *B* 熟 A から B を奪う

⑥ r ＿＿＿＿＿＿ 形 最近の

⑦ r ＿＿＿＿＿＿ 動 育てる

⑧ s ＿＿＿＿＿＿ 副 著しく

⑨ w ＿＿＿ r ＿＿＿ t ＿＿＿ ～ 熟 ～に関して

⑩ a ＿＿＿＿＿＿ 名 能力

⑪ f ＿＿＿ t ＿＿＿ *do* 熟 ～できない，～しない

⑫ c ＿＿＿＿＿＿ 動 捕まえる（= catch）

⑬ p ＿＿＿＿＿＿ 名 医師，内科医

⑭ c ＿＿＿＿＿＿ 副 創造的に，独創的に

⑮ t ＿＿＿ t ＿＿＿ *do* 熟 ～しようとする，
～しようと努める

⑯ d ＿＿＿＿＿＿ 前 ～にもかかわらず

⑰ d ＿＿＿＿＿＿ 形 耳が聞こえない

⑱ | e [   ] *A* | t [   ] *B* | 熟 | AをBに触れさせる，さらす
⑲ | l [   ] | | 形 | 言語(学)の
⑳ | i [   ] | | 名 | 孤立，分断，隔離

2. 次の[　]内の語句を並べ替えて，意味の通る英文を完成させよう。(各5点×2)

① It is almost impossible [growing / to / without / for / up / us / imagine] language.

② The ability of deaf people to learn new *words* is not affected [exposed / they / the / are / at / age / by / which] to language.

3. 次の英文を和訳してみよう。(10点)

Studies of deaf children exposed to sign language after the preschool years show that there is a critical period for grammatical development.

＊sign language「手話」　preschool year(s)「就学前の幼児期」　critical period「臨界期」

ディクテーションしてみよう！

今回学習した英文に出てきた語句・表現を，＿＿＿に書き取ろう。

🔊 43 45

43　It is almost impossible for us to ❶＿＿＿＿＿＿＿＿＿＿
＿＿＿＿＿＿ without language, which develops in our minds so effortlessly in early childhood and plays such a central role in defining us as human and allowing us ❷＿＿＿＿＿＿＿＿＿＿＿＿＿ our culture. Nevertheless, being deprived of language occasionally happens. In recent centuries children have been found living in the wild, said to have been raised by wolves or other animals and deprived of human contact. It is hard to know the real stories behind these cases, but they are all strikingly similar ❸＿＿＿
＿＿＿＿＿＿＿＿＿＿ language. The pattern is that only those rescued early in childhood developed an ability to speak. ❹＿＿＿＿＿＿＿＿＿＿
after they were about nine years old learned only a few words, or failed to learn language at all.

44   One of the most famous of these cases is that of Victor, "the wild boy of Aveyron," **❺**＿＿＿＿＿＿＿＿＿＿＿＿＿ in a film by François Truffaut called *The Wild Child*. Victor was captured in 1800, when he was about ten or eleven. He was studied by a young physician named Jean Itard, who creatively and painstakingly tried to teach him to speak, read, and write. **❻**＿＿＿＿＿＿＿＿＿＿＿ Itard's best efforts, Victor never learned to speak; he learned to read and print only a small **❼**＿＿＿＿＿＿＿＿＿＿.

45   Children without hearing are not as handicapped. A deaf child can still have language and relate normally to others **❽**＿＿＿＿＿＿＿＿＿＿
＿＿＿＿ — as long as language development starts early. There are a number of studies that show that the sooner a deaf child is exposed to a natural sign language, such as American Sign Language, the more proficient a signer he or she will become. **❾**＿＿＿＿＿＿＿＿＿＿＿
＿＿＿＿ of linguistic isolation, the ability of deaf people to learn new *words* is not affected by the age at which they are exposed to language. But their ability to learn grammar is dramatically affected. Studies of deaf children exposed to sign language after the preschool years show that there is **❿**＿＿＿＿＿＿＿＿＿＿＿＿＿＿ for grammatical development, which ends, perhaps, in the early school-age years.

確認問題の答 **1.** ① imagine   ② develop   ③ childhood   ④ define, as
⑤ deprive, of   ⑥ recent   ⑦ raise   ⑧ strikingly   ⑨ with respect to
⑩ ability   ⑪ fail to   ⑫ capture   ⑬ physician   ⑭ creatively   ⑮ try to
⑯ despite   ⑰ deaf   ⑱ expose, to   ⑲ linguistic   ⑳ isolation
2. ① for us to imagine growing up without （第1段落　第1文）
② by the age at which they are exposed （第3段落　第4文）
3. 就学前の幼児期を過ぎてから手話に触れた，耳の聞こえない子供たちに関する研究が示すところによれば，文法的発達には臨界期が存在するというのだ。 （第3段落　最終文）

ディクテーションしてみよう！の答　❶ imagine growing up   ❷ to participate in
❸ with respect to   ❹ Those found   ❺ made famous   ❻ But despite   ❼ set of words
❽ through signing   ❾ As in other cases   ❿ a critical period
アドバイス ❷ /t/ や /d/ の音が母音に挟まれると，「ら行」のような音になる（⇒フラッピング）。participate in は「パーティシペイトイン」というより「パーリシペイリン」のように聞こえる。
❾ in の /n/ の音と後ろの other の /ʌ/ の音がつながり「ナ」のように聞こえる（⇒連結）。

解 答

問1	④	問2	④	問3	②	問4	④
問5	②	問6	④	問7	②, ③		

解 説

問1

① 「ガスがないため，まったく爆発の起こらない恒星もある」
▶ 第1段落第2，3文と不一致。

② 「恒星は通常，表面上で起こる爆発は1,000に満たない」
▶ 第1段落第3文と不一致。

③ 「恒星の色は周囲で起こる爆発と関係がない」
▶ 第1段落最終文と不一致。

④ 「恒星の熱や光は，星の表面上での爆発によって生じる」
▶ 第1段落第4文と一致。

問2

① 「太陽と比較して，オレンジ色に見える恒星はずっと高温である」
▶ 第2段落最終文と不一致。

② 「恒星は太陽よりも低温だと青色に見える場合がある」
▶ 第2段落第6文と不一致。

③ 「燃焼して太陽よりもずっと高温になる恒星は存在しない」
▶ 第2段落第5文後半と不一致。

④ 「太陽よりも多くのエネルギーを生み出す恒星もある」
▶ 第2段落第5文前半と一致。

問3

　まず，下線部の turn into ～ は「～に変化する」という意味なので，③の hit と④の went around は消去できる。次に，下線部後半(主節)は，「太陽の外周部が木星の軌道を越えるだろう」とあるが，これは太陽が超巨星になった場合の大きさの説明であり，木星の軌道がすっぽり入ってしまうほどであることを

111

比喩的に述べている。以上により，②が正解とわかる。各選択肢の意味は以下のとおり。

① 「もし太陽が赤色超巨星になったら，木星は太陽から遠く離れるであろう」

② **「もし太陽が赤色超巨星に変化したら，木星の軌道は太陽の中に収まってしまうであろう」**

③ 「もし太陽が赤色超巨星に衝突したら，木星はもはや存在しなくなってしまうであろう」

④ 「もし太陽が赤色超巨星の周りを回ったら，太陽は木星に接近するであろう」

問4

① 「矮星は太陽と同程度の大きさになることはあり得ない」

▶ 第3段落第2文と不一致。太陽も矮星(dwarf)である。

② 「宇宙で最大の星の1つが太陽である」

▶ 第3段落第2文後半と不一致。もっと大きい恒星が数多く存在する，とある。

③ 「赤色超巨星は矮星の一種である」

▶ 第3段落第4文と不一致。赤色超巨星は最大級の恒星であり，他方，矮星とは小さな恒星のこと(第2段落第3文参照)である。

④ **「さまざまな大きさの星が多く存在する」**

▶ 第3段落第1文と一致。

問5

　下線部の2つのitは，いずれも太陽(our sun)を指す。主節でIt will not become a supergiant「超巨星にはならない」とあり，従属節ではその理由として，because it is not heavy enough「十分な重さ[質量]がないから」とある。よって，②が正解。各選択肢の意味は以下のとおり。

① 「太陽は，質量が増すにつれて，ゆっくりと超巨星に成長するであろう」

② **「質量のせいで，太陽は超巨星になる可能性はない」**

③ 「太陽は重いので，超巨星と同程度の大きさになり得る」

④ 「太陽は十分に質量を減らしたとき，超巨星になるであろう」

問6

① 「太陽は赤色巨星になった後，急速に冷たく暗くなる」

▶ 最終段落第3，5文および最終文と不一致。巨星になった後，まず高温になってから，ゆっくりと冷たく暗くなるのである。

② 「地球上の生物は太陽が赤色巨星になった後も生き残るであろう」

▶ 最終段落第6文と不一致。

③ 「太陽はその寿命を終えた後も光と熱を生み出し続ける」

▶ 最終段落最終文と不一致。

④ **「太陽がその寿命を終えると，地球の気温はずっと高温になるであろう」**

▶ 最終段落第5，6文と一致。

問7

① 「地球が太陽から受けるエネルギーの形態は熱と光である」

▶ 第2段落第2文と一致。

② **「地球は主として赤色超巨星によって生み出されるエネルギーによって温められている」**

▶ そのような記述はない。また，地球に熱を送る太陽は超巨星ではない（第2段落第3文）。

③ **「太陽は『黄色矮星』と呼ばれる他のすべての恒星よりもずっと大きい」**

▶ 第2段落第3文によれば，太陽自体が黄色矮星の1つなのであり，太陽が他の黄色矮星より大きいという記述はない。

④ 「白色の恒星と赤色の恒星の温度は同じではない」

▶ 第2段落第6，7文と一致。

⑤ 「宇宙空間の多くの恒星は太陽の100倍以上の大きさである」

▶ 第3段落第3文と一致。

⑥ 「太陽はこの先何百万年も存在し続けると予想されている」

▶ 最終段落第2文と一致。

⑦ 「太陽は巨星にはなり得るが超巨星にはなり得ない」

▶ 最終段落第3，4文と一致。

第1段落 文の構造と語句のチェック

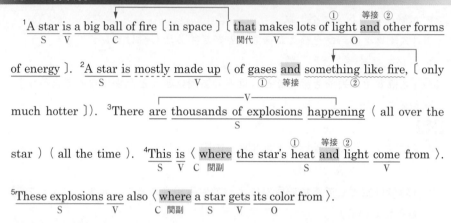

¹A star is a big ball of fire〔in space〕〔that makes lots of light and other forms
S V C 関代 V ① 等接 ② O

of energy〕. ²A star is mostly made up（of gases and something like fire,〔only
S V V ① 等接 ②

much hotter〕）. ³There are thousands of explosions happening（all over the
S

star）（all the time）. ⁴This is〈where the star's heat and light come from〉.
S V C 関副 S ① 等接 ② V

⁵These explosions are also〈where a star gets its color from〉.
S V C 関副 S V O

訳 ¹恒星とは多量の光や他の種類のエネルギーを発する，宇宙空間に浮かぶ大きな火の玉のことである。²恒星は主として，ガスや火のようなもの，ただ火よりもはるかに熱いものでできている。³常に恒星のいたるところで，何千もの爆発が起きている。⁴これが，恒星の熱や光が生じる源である。⁵これらの爆発はまた，恒星が色を得る源でもある。

Check! 第3文 There are thousands of explosions happening all over the star all the time. の There is [are] S *doing* は，S is [are] *doing*（進行形）とほぼ同じ内容。したがって，Thousands of explosions are happening all over the star all the time. と同様の意味を表すと考えてよい。同様に，There is [are] S *done* は，S is [are] *done*（受動態）とほぼ同じ内容になる。

語句

star	名	恒星，星
space	名	宇宙（空間）
light	名	光
form	名	形態，種類
energy	名	エネルギー
mostly	副	主として，大部分は

be made up of ~	熟	~から成る，~で構成される
gas	名	気体，ガス
thousands of ~	熟	何千もの~
explosion	名	爆発
all over ~	熟	~のいたるところで
all the time	熟	いつも，ずっと
heat	名	熱

第2段落　文の構造と語句のチェック

¹Our sun is a star. ²It is the closest star [to our planet], and it sends its
　　S　　V　C　　S V　　　　C　　　　　　　　　　　　　　等接　S　V

energy (to the Earth) (as heat and light). ³The sun seems large (to us), but
　O　　　　　　　　　　　　①　等接　②　　　S　　V　　C　　　　　等接

it is only a medium-sized star [called a yellow dwarf (small star)]. ⁴Other
S V　　　　　　C

stars can be different colors. ⁵Some stars have more energy (than our sun) and
　S　　V　　　C　　　　　　S　　V①　　O　　　　　　　　　等接

burn even hotter (than our sun does). ⁶Stars [that are hotter (than our sun)]
V②　　C　　　　　　　　　　　　　　S　　関代　V　　C

may look blue or white. ⁷Stars [that are cooler (than our sun)] may look
　V　　　C　　　　　S　　関代　V　　C　　　　　　　V

orange or red.
　　C

訳 ¹私たちの太陽は恒星である。²それは，私たちの惑星に最も近い恒星であり，熱や光と
してエネルギーを地球に送っている。³太陽は私たちにとっては大きく思われるが，黄色矮
星(小さな恒星)と呼ばれる中型の恒星であるに過ぎない。⁴他の恒星はさまざまな色の場合
がある。⁵私たちの太陽よりも大きなエネルギーを持ち，燃焼して太陽よりさらに高温にな
る恒星もある。⁶私たちの太陽よりも高温の恒星は，青色や白色に見える場合がある。⁷私
たちの太陽よりも低温の恒星は，オレンジ色または赤色に見える場合がある。

Check! 第5文 Some stars have more energy than our sun and burn even hotter
than our sun does. の〈even [still]＋比較級〉は「さらに，それ以上に」の意味で，
even [still] は**比較級を強調する**。これは，程度が高いものと比較して，さらに
それを上回るという意味である。なお，第1段落第2文や第3段落第2文，最
終段落第1文にある〈much [a lot / far]＋比較級〉は「ずっと，はるかに」の意
味で，差が大きいことを表す。

close	形 近い	medium-sized	形 （大きさが)中くらいの
＊活用：close-closer-closest		dwarf	名 矮星
planet	名 惑星	burn	動 燃えて～になる
		cool	形 冷えた，低温の

第3段落　文の構造と語句のチェック

¹Stars come (in many sizes). ²Our sun is about 1.4 million kilometers
S　　V　　　　　　　　　　　S　　V　　　　　　　C

around, but people still call it a dwarf (because many stars are much bigger).
　　　等接　S　　　　V　O　C　　　従接　　S　　　V　　　C

³(For example), there are many stars 〔 which are more than 100 times bigger
　　　　　　　　　　　V　　S　　　関代　V　　　　　　C

(than our sun)〕. ⁴The largest stars are called red supergiants. ⁵These stars
　　　　　　　　　　S　　　　V　　　C　　　　　　S

are so big (that most of our small solar system would fit (inside one)). ⁶(If our
V　C　従接　　　　　　　S　　　　　　　　V　　　　　　　　　従接

sun turned (into a red supergiant)), the outside of the sun would be (past
S　V　　　　　　　　　　　　　　　　S　　　　　　　V

Jupiter's orbit).

> 訳 ¹恒星には多くの大きさのものがある。²私たちの太陽は周囲がおよそ140万キロメー
> トルあるが，それでも人々は太陽を矮星と呼ぶ。なぜなら，多くの恒星が太陽よりもはる
> かに大きいからだ。³たとえば，太陽の100倍以上の大きさの恒星が数多く存在するのだ。
> ⁴最大級の恒星は赤色超巨星と呼ばれる。⁵こういった恒星は非常に大きいので，私たちの
> 小さな太陽系のほとんどが，そういった恒星の中に収まってしまうほどだ。⁶もし私たちの
> 太陽が赤色超巨星に変化するとしたら，太陽の外周部は木星の軌道を越えてしまうであろ
> う。

Check! 第5文 These stars are so big that most of our small solar system would fit inside one. は〈so ～ that ...〉構文「とても～なので…」になっており，that 以下で助動詞 would が使われているのは，仮定法の意味を表すため。実際に太陽系が恒星の中に入るわけではないが，大きさの面ですっぽり入ってしまうほどである，という内容。文末の one は one of these stars と考えればよい。

語 句

come in ～	熟	～の種類[形式]がある
size	名	大きさ
million	形	百万の
kilometer	名	キロメートル
around	副	周囲で，一周すると
still	副	それでも(なお)
supergiant	名	超巨星

solar system	名	太陽系
inside	前	～の中に，～の内側に
turn into ～	熟	～に変わる，～に変化する
outside	名	外側
past	前	～を過ぎて，～を越えて
Jupiter	名	木星
orbit	名	軌道

第4段落　文の構造と語句のチェック

¹Stars, (just like people), have a life, but a star's life is much longer (than a human's life).　²The sun is millions of years old and will live (for many more millions of years).　³(When our sun starts to die), it will grow (into a red giant star).　⁴It will not become a supergiant (because it is not heavy enough).　⁵(When our sun dies), it will get so hot (that the heat and light will burn the Earth).　⁶(In fact), it will be too hot (for anything to live (on the Earth)) (when our sun becomes a red giant).　⁷Then, our sun will slowly get darker and colder (until it stops 〈 giving off any energy 〉(at all)).

117

訳 ¹恒星には人間とちょうど同じように，寿命がある。だが，恒星の寿命は人間の寿命よりずっと長い。²太陽はできてから何百万年もたっており，これからもさらに何百万年も存続するだろう。³太陽が終わりを迎えようとすると，赤色巨星へと変化を遂げるであろう。⁴太陽は超巨星にはならない。なぜなら，十分な質量がないからだ。⁵太陽が死ぬとき，非常に熱くなるので，その熱と光で地球は燃やされてしまうであろう。⁶実際，太陽が赤色巨星になると，あまりに熱くなるため，いかなるものも地球上で生きられなくなるであろう。⁷その後，太陽はゆっくりと暗く，冷たくなり，ついにはまったくエネルギーを発しなくなるだろう。

Check! 最終段落最終文の until の意味のとり方に注意しよう。基本的に，接続詞 until [till] は，「…するまで」の意味であるが，until [till] の導く節が主節より後に置かれるとき，「ついに…」という意味で理解するとわかりやすい場合がある。たとえば，「疲れるまで働き続けた」と「働き続けてついに疲れてしまった」は同様の意味である。本文も，「まったくエネルギーを発しなくなるまでゆっくりと暗く冷たくなってゆく」ととらえてもよいが，「ゆっくりと暗く冷たくなってゆき，ついにはまったくエネルギーを発しなくなる」と理解したほうがわかりやすい。

語句

life	名	生命，寿命
millions of ~	熟	何百万もの~
grow into ~	熟	~へと成長[発達]する
giant	形	巨大な／名 巨大なもの
burn	動	燃やす，燃焼する
slowly	副	ゆっくりと
until	接	~するまで(ずっと)
stop *doing*	熟	~するのをやめる，~しなくなる
give off ~	熟	~を発する，放つ
at all	熟	(否定文で)まったく(~ない)

文法事項の整理 ⑩　仮定法の基本パターン

第3段落最終文をみてみよう。

If our sun **turned** into a red supergiant, the outside of the sun **would be** past Jupiter's orbit.

■仮定法の形

事実に反することを仮定する表現方法を【**仮定法**】という。これに対し，事実をそのまま述べるのは【**直説法**】という。

　仮定法の特徴は，現在の内容が過去形，過去の内容が過去完了形で書かれる，つまり，通常の文（＝直説法）と比べて時制が1つ前にずれる点だ。

① 例　If I were rich, I could buy the house.
　　　「（今）私が金持ちなら，（今）その家を買えるのだが」
　　　→現実は，金持ちでないから買えない。
　　　　（≒ As I am not rich, I can't buy the house.）

② 例　If I had been rich, I could have bought the house.
　　　「（あのとき）私が金持ちだったら，（あのとき）その家を買えたのだが」
　　　→現実は，金持ちでなかったから買えなかった。
　　　　（≒ As I was not rich, I couldn't buy the house.）

③ 例　If I had worked hard, I could buy the house.
　　　「（あのとき）熱心に働いていたら，（今）その家を買えるのだが」
　　　→現実は，熱心に働かなかったから買えない。
　　　　（≒ As I did not work hard, I can't buy the house.）

　パターンを整理すると以下のようになる。

If＋S＋動詞の過去形〜 ──①─→ S＋助動詞の過去形＋do ...
（今）S が〜すれば　　　　　③　　（今）S は…するだろう
If＋S＋had done 〜 ──②─→ S＋助動詞の過去形＋have done ...
（あのとき）S が〜したら　　　　（あのとき）S は…しただろう
（①②③は，上の例文に対応）

　①のパターンを【仮定法過去】，②のパターンを【仮定法過去完了】という。③は①＋②の混合である。

■第3段落最終文

If our sun turned into a red supergiant, the outside of the sun would be past Jupiter's orbit.

▶ ①のパターン（仮定法過去）になっている。

確認問題

1. 次の和訳と対応する英語の語句を，頭文字を参考にして書き，空欄を完成させよう。

（各1点×20）

①	l		名	光
②	f		名	形態，種類
③	e		名	エネルギー
④	m		副	主として，大部分は
⑤	be	m　u　o	〜	熟 〜から成る，〜で構成される
⑥	t　　o		〜	熟 何千もの〜
⑦	e		名	爆発
⑧	a　　t　　t		熟	いつも，ずっと
⑨	h		名	熱
⑩	c		形	近い
⑪	p		名	惑星
⑫	c		形	冷えた，低温の
⑬	s		名	大きさ
⑭	s　　s		名	太陽系
⑮	i		前	〜の中に，〜の内側に
⑯	t　　i		〜	熟 〜に変わる，〜に変化する
⑰	p		前	〜を過ぎて，〜を越えて
⑱	o		名	軌道
⑲	m　　o		〜	熟 何百万もの〜
⑳	g　　o		〜	熟 〜を発する，放つ

2. 次の[　]内の語句を並べ替えて，意味の通る英文を完成させよう。（各5点×2）

① A star is mostly [something / of / gases / up / made / and] like fire, only much hotter.

120

② When our sun dies, it will [heat / that / hot / so / the / get] and light will burn the Earth.

3. 次の英文を和訳してみよう。(10点)

If our sun turned into a red supergiant, the outside of the sun would be past Jupiter's orbit.

＊supergiant「超巨星」　Jupiter「木星」

ディクテーションしてみよう！

今回学習した英文に出てきた語句・表現を，＿＿＿に書き取ろう。

47・50

47　A star is a big ball of fire in space that makes ❶＿＿＿＿＿＿＿＿＿ ＿＿ and other forms of energy.　A star is mostly made up of gases and something like fire, only much hotter.　There are thousands of explosions happening all over the star all the time.　This is where the star's heat and light come from.　These explosions are also ❷＿＿＿＿＿＿＿＿＿＿＿ ＿＿ its color from.

48　Our sun is a star.　It is the ❸＿＿＿＿＿＿＿＿＿ to our planet, and it sends its energy to the Earth as heat and light.　The sun seems large to us, but it is only a medium-sized star called a yellow dwarf (small star). Other stars can be different colors.　Some stars have more energy than our sun and burn even hotter than our sun does.　Stars that are hotter than our sun may look blue or white.　Stars that are cooler than our sun may look ❹＿＿＿＿＿＿＿＿＿＿＿.

49　Stars come in many sizes.　Our sun is about ❺＿＿＿＿＿＿＿＿＿ kilometers around, but people still call it a dwarf because many stars are much bigger.　For example, there are many stars which are more than 100 times bigger than our sun.　The largest stars are called red supergiants. These stars are so big that most of our small solar system would ❻＿＿＿＿ ＿＿＿＿＿＿＿＿.　If our sun ❼＿＿＿＿＿＿＿＿＿ a red supergiant, the outside of the sun would be past Jupiter's orbit.

50　Stars, just like people, have a life, but a star's life is much longer than a human's life. The sun is millions of years old and will live for many more millions of years. When our sun starts to die, it will grow into a red giant star. It will not become a supergiant because it is not ❽_____ _____. When our sun dies, it will get so hot that the heat and light will burn the Earth. In fact, it will be too hot ❾_____ _____ to live on the Earth when our sun becomes a red giant. Then, our sun will slowly get darker and colder until it stops ❿_____ any energy at all.

確認問題の答　**1.** ① light　② form　③ energy　④ mostly　⑤ made up of
⑥ thousands of　⑦ explosion　⑧ all the time　⑨ heat　⑩ close
⑪ planet　⑫ cool　⑬ size　⑭ solar system　⑮ inside
⑯ turn into　⑰ past　⑱ orbit　⑲ millions of　⑳ give off
2. ① made up of gases and something　（第 1 段落　第 2 文）
② get so hot that the heat　（第 4 段落　第 5 文）
3. もし私たちの太陽が赤色超巨星に変化するとしたら，太陽の外周部は木星の軌道を越えてしまうであろう。
（第 3 段落　最終文）

ディクテーションしてみよう！の答　❶ lots of light　❷ where a star gets　❸ closest star
❹ orange or red　❺ 1.4 million　❻ fit inside one　❼ turned into
❽ heavy enough　❾ for anything　❿ giving off
アドバイス　❸ close は動詞の場合 /klouz/ だが，形容詞の場合の発音は /klous/。最上級は /klóusest/ となる。
❿単語の末尾に破裂音（/p/，/t/，/k/，/b/，/d/，/g/ の音）があるとほとんど発音されない（⇒脱落）。giving
の末尾の g はほぼ発音されず，その前の /n/ の音が後続の off とつながり（⇒連結），「ギヴィノフ」のように
聞こえる。

11 解答・解説

問題は別冊 p.42

解 答

問1	④	問2	④	問3	②	問4	③
問5	②	問6	④	問7	①	問8	③
問9	①	問10	②				

解 説

問1

① 「体重の変化について，世論調査の参加者に気分良く思わせるため」

② 「これらの成人の中にはパンデミック前に減量を計画していた人がいたため」

③ 「体重の変化を経験した成人は，自分の体型に完全に満足していたため」

④ **「偶発的な体重変化と意図的な体重変化の違いを強調するため」**

▶ 第5段落から，パンデミック時の体重変化の要因はストレスだとわかる。ここから undesired「望ましくない」は，体重変化が，美容目的など自らが意図したものではなく，ストレスという外的要因によるものであることを明確にしていると考え，④を選ぶ。

問2

空欄の直前では望ましくない体重増加をした人の割合，空欄の直後では望ましくない体重減少をした人の割合が書かれている。ここから，前後が対比されていると考えて，④「その反面」を選ぶ。

① 「一方で」

▶ on (the) one hand は以下のように用いる。

例 On (the) one hand, ○○○. On the other hand, ×××.
「一方では，○○○。他方では，×××」

この形で，「○○○」と「×××」が対比される。on the other hand は単独で用いることが多いが，on (the) one hand は on the other hand とセットでしか使えない。本問では，on the other hand であれば正解となりうる。

② 「結局」

▶ 文意に合わない。

③「〜に加えて」

▶ 副詞の働きをする in addition「加えて」であれば正解となりうる。in addition to 〜 は前置詞の働きをし，「〜」の部分には名詞が入る。

問3

①「多くのアメリカ人が食べ過ぎによる体重増加を経験した」

▶「食べ過ぎ」についての言及はない。

②**「パンデミック時に多くのアメリカ人が体重の変化を経験したことが研究で明らかになった」**

▶ 第1段落第2文と一致。

③「どちらの研究も，2020年2月から6月までの体重変化を調べた」

▶ 第1，2段落で紹介されているアメリカ心理学会の世論調査については，調査時期が述べられていない。よって不適。

④「調査によれば，パンデミック時には，体重の増加よりも減少を経験する人が多かった」

▶ 第2段落によれば，体重増加が42%，体重減少が18%近くなので，誤り。

問4

　下線部(**ウ**)の diet は lifestyle と並べられているので，「(日々の)食事」の意味。

①「私の友人のアリソンは，月末に健康診断を受けるのでダイエットしている」

▶ 日本語の「ダイエット」に近い，「(美容や治療目的で)ダイエットをする」の意味。動詞として用いている。

②「議員たちは何週間も国会で移民法の改正を議論している」

▶「国会，議会」の意味。the Diet と D を大文字で表記する。

③**「健康維持のために守るべき習慣には，定期的な運動と健康的な食事がある」**

▶「(日々の)食事」の意味。

④「このテレビ局は，悪趣味なリアリティー番組と料理番組だけを大量に流している」

▶ a diet of 〜 で「大量の〜」の意味。

問5

　下線部(エ)innate は「生まれつきの，生得的な」の意味。仮に知らなくても，文後半の that evolved as a survival mechanism「生存の仕組みとして進化した」からある程度推測できるだろう。② natural には「自然な，天然の，当然の」のほか，「生まれつきの」の意味がある。他の選択肢の意味は，①「予想された」，③「すばやい」，④「透明な」。

問6

　①「人間はストレスの多い状況に直面すると，外見により気を配り始める」

　▶「外見に気を配る」という記述はない。

　②「過度のストレスにより，脳が生成するセロトニンやドーパミンなどの神経伝達物質の量が増える」

　▶第7段落第1文と不一致。これらの物質のレベル［値］が下がると書かれている。

　③「パンデミックに比べ，食糧不足や捕食動物との遭遇は，人々をより深刻なストレスにさらす」

　▶そのような比較はなされていない。第6段落第2文で「食糧不足」は慢性のストレス，「捕食動物」は急性のストレスの例として挙げられているが，いずれも「闘争・逃走反応」の説明の一部であり，パンデミックと直接的な関係はない。

　④「ストレスの多い状況で活性化される脳の仕組みが，不健康な習慣につながる可能性がある」

　▶第7段落全体の内容と一致。

問7

　直後の文で食べ物の具体例として挙げられている chocolate and other sweets「チョコレートなどの甘い菓子」がどんな食べ物かを考える。同段落最終文にある low-nutrient, calorie-dense food「低栄養・高カロリー食」などから①「高カロリーの」を選ぶ。他の選択肢の意味は，②「甘酸っぱい」，③「既製品の」，④「自己管理の」。

　直前の What about weight loss? は，第9段落の「なぜ人々の体重が増減したか」という問いかけを受けたもので，「なぜ人々の体重が減ったのか」ということ。下線部以降で体重減少の仕組みが端的に説明されているので，③の In short「簡潔に言えば」が適切と判断する。nutshell は「木の実の殻」が原義で「小さいもの」の比喩として用いられ，in a nutshell で「簡潔に言えば，要するに」の意味。他の選択肢の意味は，①「ある程度」，②「協同で，協力して」，④「長い目で見れば，長期的には」。

①「高カロリーの食品を食べると，（食べる）前より幸せな気分になるかもしれないが，その気分は長く続かない」

▶ 第10段落第2，3文と一致。本文の the mental boost is extremely short-lived「精神的な高揚は極めて短命で終わる」が，選択肢の the feeling doesn't last long「その（幸せな）気分は長く続かない」に言い換えられている点に注目しよう。

②「迷走神経を通る信号が強くなると，人々は食欲を失うことがある」

▶ 第11段落第3，4文によれば，信号が抑制された結果，満腹感を感じる（≒食欲を失う）ので，一致しない。

③「体重が増えるか減るかは，脳の仕組みとは関係ない」

▶ 第10段落は体重増加，第11段落は体重減少について，それぞれ脳の仕組みとの関係を説明している。

④「パンデミックによる余分なストレスが，家庭でのたくさんの気晴らしと組み合わされて，望ましくない体重変化の主な原因となった」

▶ 第12段落第1文と不一致。たくさんあったのは「食べ物」であり，「気晴らし」はほとんどなかったと書かれている。

問10

① 「極端にストレスの多い状況では，人々は食べ過ぎるよりも，食べるのをやめてしまう可能性が高い」

▶ ストレスのある状況で食べ過ぎる仕組みを第10段落，食べなくなる仕組みを第11段落で述べているが，どちらの可能性が高いか，という比較はされていない。

② **「ストレスの多い状況がもたらす望ましくない結果を避けるために，ポジティブな独り言など，ストレスを軽減する代わりの方法を試すべきである」**

▶ 最終段落最終文と一致。

③ 「闘争・逃走反応は，パンデミック中の望ましくない体重変化の原因として大きな役割を果たしてはいない」

▶ 第5段落以降で，パンデミックにおける体重変化の原因の説明として，ストレスに対する身体の反応＝闘争・逃走反応を挙げている。したがって，大きな役割を果たしていると考えられる。

④ 「体重を管理する必要があるときは，自分自身にストレスを与えることで闘争・逃走反応を作用させるべきだ」

▶ 第5段落以降で，闘争・逃走反応は望ましくない体重変化を引き起こすものとして説明されているので不適。

それでは次に，段落ごとに詳しくみていこう。

51

第1段落　文の構造と語句のチェック

¹(If you have experienced unwanted weight gain or weight loss (during the
　従接 S　　V　　　　　　　①　　　　　　　等接 ②　　　　　　O

pandemic)), you are not alone.　²(According to a poll 〔 by the American
　　　　　　　S　V　　C

Psychological Association 〕), 61% of U.S. adults reported undesired weight
　　　　　　　　　　　　　　　　　S　　　　　V　　　　O

change (since the pandemic began).
　　　　　従接　　S　　　V

> **訳** ¹もしパンデミック中に望ましくない体重増加や体重減少を経験したとしたら，それは
> あなただけではない。²アメリカ心理学会の世論調査によると，パンデミックが始まって以
> 降，アメリカの成人の61％が望ましくない体重変化を報告した。

語句

experience	動 経験する	**pandemic**	名 パンデミック（病気の世界的流行）
unwanted	形 望ましくない	**poll**	名 世論調査，意識調査
weight gain	名 体重増加	**undesired**	形 望ましくない
weight loss	名 体重減少		

第2段落　文の構造と語句のチェック

¹The results, (released in March 2021), showed 〈 that (during the
　S　　　　　　　　　　　　　　　　　　V　O　従接

pandemic), 42% of respondents gained unwanted weight — 29 pounds on
　　　　　　　S　　　　　　　V　　　O

average — and nearly 10% of those people gained more than 50 pounds 〉.　²(On
　　　　　等接　　　　S　　　　　　　V　　　　O

128

従接 that 省略

the flip side), nearly 18% of Americans said 〈 they experienced unwanted
　　　　　　　　　　　　　S　　　　　　　　V　　O　 S　　　　　V　　　　　　　O

weight loss — on average, a loss of 26 pounds 〉.

> **訳** ¹以上の調査結果は，2021 年 3 月に発表されたが，パンデミック中，回答者の 42%が望ましくない体重増加（平均 29 ポンド）をしており，その人々の 10%近くが 50 ポンド以上増加したことを示していた。²その反面，18%近くのアメリカ人が望ましくない体重減少（平均で 26 ポンドの減少）を経験したと回答した。

語句

release	動 発表する	
respondent	名 回答者	
gain	動 増量する，増加する	
gain weight	熟 体重が増加する	

pound	名 ポンド（重量の単位）
on average	熟 平均して
on the flip side	熟 一方で，その反面
loss	名 減量，減少

第 3 段落　文の構造と語句のチェック

¹Another study, (published on March 22, 2021), assessed weight change in
　S　　　　　　　　　　　　　　　　　　　　　　　　　　　V　　　　　O

269 people (from February to June 2020). ²The researchers found, (on average),
　　　　　　　　　　　　　　　　　　　　　　　　　　　S　　　　　　V

〈 that people gained a steady 1.5 pounds (per month)〉.
O 従接　 S　　　 V　　　　　　O

> **訳** ¹2021 年 3 月 22 日に発表された別の研究では，2020 年 2 月から 6 月までの 269 人の体重変化を評価した。²研究者たちは平均して 1 カ月に 1.5 ポンドずつ着実に人々の体重が増加していることを発見した。

語句

publish	動 公表する，発表する
assess	動 評価する，査定する

researcher	名 研究者
steady	形 一定の，着実な
per	前 ～につき，～ごとに

第4段落　文の構造と語句のチェック

¹I am a nutritional neuroscientist, and my research investigates the
S V C 　等接 S V

relationship 〔 between diet, lifestyle, stress and mental distress 〔 such as
O

anxiety and depression 〕〕.
① 　等接 　②

> **訳** ¹私は栄養神経科学者で，私の研究では，食事，ライフスタイル，ストレスと，不安や
> うつなどの精神的苦痛との関係を調査している。

語句

nutritional	形 栄養の		**relationship**	名 関係	
neuroscientist	名 神経科学者		**diet**	名 （日々の）食事	
research	名 研究		**distress**	名 苦痛，疲労	
investigate	動 調査する		**anxiety**	名 不安，心配	
			depression	名 うつ(病)	

第5段落　文の構造と語句のチェック

¹The common denominator 〔 to changes 〔 in body weight 〕, 〔 especially during
S

a pandemic 〕〕, is stress. ²The findings 〔 about unwanted weight changes 〕 make
V C S V

sense (in a stressful world), (especially in the context of the body's stress
O

response, 〔 better known as the fight-or-flight response 〕).

> **訳** ¹特にパンデミック時の体重の変化に共通する要素はストレスだ。²望ましくない体重の
> 変化に関する調査結果は，ストレスの多い世界では，特に闘争・逃走反応としてよりよく
> 知られている，身体のストレス反応との関連で，納得できるものだ。

語句

common	形	共通の
denominator	名	(共通の)要素，特徴
especially	副	特に
finding	名	調査結果
make sense	熟	道理にかなう，理解できる
stressful	形	ストレスの多い

in the context of ～
熟 ～との関連で，～という状況下において
response 名 反応
better known as ～
熟 ～という呼称の方がよく知られて
fight-or-flight 形 戦うか逃げるかの

第6段落 文の構造と語句のチェック

¹The fight-or-flight response(S) is(V) an innate reaction(C) 〔that(関代) evolved(V) (as a survival mechanism)〕. ²It(S) empowers(V) humans(O) 〔to react swiftly to acute stress(C) — 〔like a predator〕①— or(等接) adapt to chronic stress — 〔like a food shortage〕②〕. ³(When(従接) — the body is 省略 — faced with stress), the body(S) wants(V) to keep(O) the brain(C) alert. ⁴It(S) decreases(V) levels(O) 〔of some hormones(①) and(等接) brain chemicals(②)〕(in order to turn down behaviors 〔that(関代) won't help(V) (in an urgent situation))〕), and(等接) it(S) increases(V) other hormones(O) 〔that(関代) will(V)〕.
— help in an urgent situation 省略

訳 ¹闘争・逃走反応は，生存の仕組みとして進化した生得的な反応である。²そのおかげで人間は急性のストレス(たとえば捕食動物)にすばやく反応し，慢性のストレス(たとえば食糧不足)に順応する力を備えている。³ストレスに直面したとき，身体は脳が警戒した状態を維持することを望む。⁴緊急事態に役立たない行動を抑えるために，一部のホルモンや脳内化学物質のレベルが下がり，役立つ他のホルモンが増える。

第7段落　文の構造と語句のチェック

the body is 省略

¹(When under stress), the body lowers levels (of neurotransmitters (such as
　　従接　　　　　　　　　S　　　　V　　　O

serotonin, dopamine and melatonin)). ²Serotonin regulates emotions, appetite
　　①　　　　　②　　　等接　　③　　　　　　S　　　V　　①　　②　　O

and digestion. ³So, low levels of serotonin increase anxiety and can change a
等接　③　　　　　　等接　　　　S　　　　　　　　V①　　　O　　等接　　V②

person's eating habits. ⁴Dopamine — another feel-good neurotransmitter —
　　　O　　　　　　　　　　S　└──同格──┘

regulates goal-oriented motivation. ⁵Dwindling levels of dopamine can translate
　　V　　　　　　O　　　　　　　　　　　S　　　　　　　　　　　V

(into lower motivation (to exercise, maintain a healthy lifestyle or perform
　　　　　　　　　　　　　①　　　　　②　　　　　　　　　　等接　③

daily tasks)).

132

訳 ¹ストレスがかかると，身体はセロトニン，ドーパミン，メラトニンなどの神経伝達物質のレベルを下げる。²セロトニンは，感情，食欲，消化を調節している。³そのため，セロトニンのレベルが低いと不安が増し，人の食習慣を変えてしまう可能性がある。⁴ドーパミン（もう1つの快感をもたらす神経伝達物質）は目標志向のモチベーションを調節する。⁵ドーパミンのレベルが低下すると，運動をしたり健康的なライフスタイルを維持したり日課を行うモチベーションが低下するといった結果につながる場合がある。

語句

lower	動 低下させる
neurotransmitter	名 神経伝達物質
serotonin	名 セロトニン
dopamine	名 ドーパミン
melatonin	名 メラトニン
regulate	動 調節する
emotion	名 感情
appetite	名 食欲
digestion	名 消化

goal-oriented	形 目標志向の
motivation	名 モチベーション，動機付け
dwindle	動 減少する，低下する
translate into ~	熟 ~に転化される，~という結果に結びつく
exercise	動 運動する
maintain	動 維持する
perform	動 行う
task	名 作業，任務

第8段落　文の構造と語句のチェック

¹(Overall), <u>stress</u> <u>can throw</u> your <u>eating habits</u> and <u>motivation</u> [to exercise
S (V) (①) 等接 (②) (①)

or eat healthy] (way out of balance), and <u>this last year</u> <u>has</u> certainly <u>been</u> a
等接② 等接 S V

<u>stressful one</u> (for everyone).
C

訳 ¹全体として，ストレスは食習慣や運動・健康的な食事へのモチベーションのバランスを大幅に乱す可能性があり，ここ最近の1年は間違いなく誰にとってもストレスの多い年であった。

語句

overall	副 全体として，全体的に言って
throw ~ out of balance	熟 ~のバランスを失わせる，乱す
eat healthy	熟 身体に良いものを食べる，健康的な食事をする
way	副 はるかに，遠くに

第9段落　文の構造と語句のチェック

¹So why did people gain or lose weight (this last year)? ²And what explains
等接　　（V）　S　　V　　　O　　　　　　　　　　　　　等接　S　　　V

the dramatic differences?
O

> **訳** ¹では，なぜ人々はここ最近の 1 年で体重が増減したのだろうか。²そして，劇的な違い
> は何によって説明がつくのだろうか。

語句

dramatic 形 劇的な

第10段落　文の構造と語句のチェック

¹Many people find comfort (in high-calorie food). ²That is (because chocolate
S　　　V　　O　　　　　　　　　　　　　　　　　　S　　V　　従接

and other sweets can make you happy (by boosting serotonin levels) (in the
S　　　　　V　　O　　C

short term)). ³However, the blood clears the extra sugar (very quickly), so the
S　　　V　　　O　　　　　　　　　　　　　等接

mental boost is extremely short-lived, (leading people to eat more). ⁴〈 Eating
S　　V　　　C　　　　　　　　V'　　O'　　C'　　　　　　S

for comfort 〉can be a natural response 〔 to stress 〕, but (when combined with
V　　　C　　　　　　　　　　　等接　　従接

the lower motivation to exercise and consumption of low-nutrient, calorie-dense
①　　　　　　　等接　　　　　②

food), stress can result in unwanted weight gain.
S　　V　　　　O

> 訳 ¹多くの人は，高カロリーの食べ物に安らぎを見出す。²その理由は，チョコレートなどの甘い菓子は，短期的にはセロトニンレベルを高めて幸せな気分にさせてくれるからである。³しかし，血液中の余分な糖分はすぐに排出されるため，精神的な高揚は極めて短命で終わり，結果として人々がもっと食べたくなるようになる。⁴安らぎを求めて食べることは，ストレスに対する自然な反応と言えるが，運動意欲の低下や低栄養・高カロリー食の摂取と結びつくと，ストレスは望ましくない体重増加につながる可能性がある。

語句

comfort	名	安らぎ，安楽
high-calorie	形	高カロリーの
chocolate	名	チョコレート
sweet	名	甘いもの，甘い菓子
boost	動	高める，増大させる／
	名	高まり，増大
in the short term	熟	短期的には，短期間に
blood	名	血液
clear	動	取り除く，排除する

extra	形	余分な
extremely	副	非常に，極端に
short-lived	形	短命の
combine	動	組み合わせる，結びつける
▶combine A with B		
	熟	A を B と結びつける
consumption	名	摂取
low-nutrient	形	栄養価の低い
calorie-dense	形	高カロリーの
result in ~	熟	～という結果につながる

第11段落 文の構造と語句のチェック

¹What about weight loss? ²(In a nutshell), the brain is connected (to the
　　　　　　　　　　　　　　　　　　　　S　　V　　C

gut)(through a two-way communication system 〔called the vagus nerve 〕).

³(When you are stressed), your body inhibits the signals 〔 that travel (through
　従接　S　V　　C　　　　　S　　　V①　　　O　　関代　V

the vagus nerve)〕 and slows down the digestive process. ⁴(When this
　　　　　　　　　　等接　V②　　　　O　　　　　　　従接　S

happens), people experience fullness.
　V　　　　S　　　V　　　O

> 訳 ¹体重減少についてはどうだろうか。²簡潔に言えば，脳は迷走神経と呼ばれる双方向伝達システムを通じて腸とつながっている。³ストレスを感じると，身体は迷走神経を伝わる信号を抑制し，消化のプロセスを遅らせる。⁴これが起こると，人は満腹感を体験する。

語句

in a nutshell	熟	簡潔に言えば，要するに
be connected to ~	熟	～とつながっている
gut	名	腸
two-way	形	双方向の
vagus nerve	名	迷走神経
stressed	形	ストレスを感じて
inhibit	動	抑制する，妨害する
signal	名	信号，シグナル
slow down	熟	遅くする
digestive	形	消化の
fullness	名	満腹感

第12段落　文の構造と語句のチェック

¹The pandemic left many people confined to their homes, bored and (with
S　　　　　　V　　　　O　　　　confined to their homes C①　　bored C②　等接

plenty of food and little to distract them). ²(When adding the stress factor to
①　　等接　　②　　　　　　　　従接

this scenario), you have a perfect situation [for unwanted weight changes].
S　　V　　　O

　　　　　　　　　　　　　　　　　　　　　　　関代 which 省略

³Stress will always be a part of life, but there are things [you can do] — (like
S　　　V　　C　等接　　　V　　S　　S　V

　　　　　　　　　　to 省略

practicing positive self-talk) — [that can help ⟨ ward off the stress response
関代　　V　　O　　　　　　①

and some of its unwanted consequences ⟩].
等接　　　②

訳 ¹パンデミックのせいで多くの人が，退屈で，食べ物がたくさんあり，気晴らしがほとんどない状態で家に引きこもった。²この事態にストレスの要因が加わると，望ましくない体重変化には申し分ない状況になる。³ストレスは常に生活の一部だが，ポジティブな独り言を実践するなど，実行可能なことで，ストレス反応やその望ましくない結果を回避する助けとなるようなことも存在する。

語句

be confined to ~	熟	～に引きこもって，閉じこもって
distract	動	気を紛らす，気晴らしになる
factor	名	要因，要素
scenario	名	筋書き，事態
self-talk	名	独り言，つぶやき
ward off	熟	避ける，回避する
consequence	名	結果

文法事項の整理 ⑪　関係詞の二重限定

第12段落最終文の that についてみてみよう。

Stress will always be a part of life, but there are things you can do — like practicing positive self-talk — **that** can help ward off the stress response and some of its unwanted consequences.

　2つの関係詞節が二重に先行詞を修飾[限定]することがある。〈目的格＋目的格〉と〈目的格＋主格〉のパターンが多く，前の目的格の関係代名詞は省略されることが多い。

例　Is there *anything* you want which you don't have?

　　「あなたが欲しいもので，持っていないものはありますか」
　＊(that) you want が1つ目，which you don't have が2つ目。それぞれ anything を修飾している。〈目的格＋目的格〉パターン。

例　He is the only *student* I know who can speak French.

　　「彼は私が知っている中で，フランス語を話せる唯一の学生だ」
　＊(that) I know が1つ目，who can speak French が2つ目。それぞれ student を修飾している。〈目的格＋主格〉パターン。

■第12段落最終文
Stress will always be a part of life, but there are things you can do — like practicing positive self-talk — that can help ward off the stress response and some of its unwanted consequences.

▶ (which) you can do が1つ目，that can ～ consequences が2つ目。それぞれ things を修飾している。〈目的格＋主格〉パターン。

確認問題

1. 次の和訳と対応する英語の語句を，頭文字を参考にして書き，空欄を完成させよう。

（各1点×20）

No.	頭文字	品詞	和訳
①	e	動	経験する
②	o　　　a	熟	平均して
③	a	動	評価する，査定する
④	r	名	研究者
⑤	s	形	一定の，着実な
⑥	d	名	(日々の)食事
⑦	a	名	不安，心配
⑧	d	名	うつ(病)
⑨	c	形	共通の
⑩	m　　　s	熟	道理にかなう，理解できる
⑪	e	動	進化する
⑫	s	名	生存，生き残り
⑬	a	形	急性の
⑭	c	形	慢性の
⑮	u	形	緊急の
⑯	a	名	食欲
⑰	m	動	維持する
⑱	e	副	非常に，極端に
⑲	c	名	摂取
⑳	f	名	要因，要素

2. 次の[　]内の語句を並べ替えて，意味の通る英文を完成させよう。（各5点×2）

① If [have / weight / experienced / you / unwanted / gain] or weight loss
during the pandemic, you are not alone.

② When faced with stress, the body [brain / to / keep / wants / the] alert.

3. 次の英文を和訳してみよう。(10点)

There are things you can do that can help ward off the stress response and some of its unwanted consequences.

＊ward off「避ける，回避する」

ディクテーションしてみよう！

今回学習した英文に出てきた語句・表現を，＿＿＿に書き取ろう。

52 / 63

52　If you have experienced unwanted weight gain or weight loss during the pandemic, ❶＿＿＿＿＿＿＿＿＿＿＿＿＿＿＿. According to a poll by the American Psychological Association, 61% of U.S. adults reported undesired weight change since the pandemic began.

53　The results, released in March 2021, showed that during the pandemic, 42% of respondents gained unwanted weight — 29 pounds on average — and nearly 10% of those people gained more than ❷＿＿＿＿＿ pounds.　On the flip side, nearly 18% of Americans said they experienced unwanted weight loss — on average, a loss of 26 pounds.

54　Another study, published on March 22, 2021, assessed weight change in 269 people from February to June 2020.　The researchers found, on average, that people gained ❸＿＿＿＿＿＿＿＿＿＿＿＿＿＿＿＿＿＿＿＿.

55　I am a nutritional neuroscientist, and my research investigates the relationship between diet, lifestyle, stress and mental distress such as ❹＿＿＿＿＿＿＿＿＿＿＿＿＿＿＿＿＿.

56　The common denominator to changes in body weight, especially during a pandemic, is stress.　The findings about unwanted weight changes make sense in a stressful world, especially in the context of the body's stress response, better known as the fight-or-flight response.

57   The fight-or-flight response ❺_____

_____ that evolved as a survival mechanism.   It empowers humans to react swiftly to acute stress — like a predator — or adapt to chronic stress — like a food shortage.   When faced with stress, the body wants to keep the brain alert.   It decreases levels of some hormones and brain chemicals in order to turn down behaviors that won't help in an urgent situation, and it increases other hormones ❻_____.

58   When under stress, the body lowers levels of neurotransmitters such as serotonin, dopamine and melatonin.   Serotonin regulates emotions, appetite and digestion.   So, low levels of serotonin increase anxiety and can change a person's eating habits.   Dopamine — another feel-good neurotransmitter — regulates goal-oriented motivation.   Dwindling levels of dopamine can translate into lower motivation to exercise, ❼_____ _____ or perform daily tasks.

59   Overall, stress can throw your eating habits and motivation to exercise or eat healthy way out of balance, and this last year has certainly been a stressful one for everyone.

60   So why did people gain or lose weight this last year?   And what explains the dramatic differences?

61   Many people find comfort in high-calorie food.   That is because chocolate and other sweets can make you happy by boosting serotonin levels in the short term.   However, the blood clears the extra sugar very quickly, so the mental boost is extremely short-lived, leading people to eat more. Eating for comfort can be a natural response to stress, but ❽_____ _____ the lower motivation to exercise and consumption of low-nutrient, calorie-dense food, stress can result in unwanted weight gain.

62   ❾_____ weight loss?   In a nutshell, the brain is connected to the gut through a two-way communication system called the vagus nerve.   When you are stressed, your body inhibits the signals that travel through the vagus nerve and slows down the digestive process. When this happens, people experience fullness.

63　　The pandemic left many people confined to their homes, bored and with plenty of food and little to distract them. When adding the stress factor to this scenario, you have a perfect situation for unwanted weight changes. Stress will always ❿_____, but there are things you can do — like practicing positive self-talk — that can help ward off the stress response and some of its unwanted consequences.

確認問題の答　1.　① experience　② on average　③ assess　④ researcher　⑤ steady
　　⑥ diet　⑦ anxiety　⑧ depression　⑨ common　⑩ make sense　⑪ evolve
　　⑫ survival　⑬ acute　⑭ chronic　⑮ urgent　⑯ appetite　⑰ maintain
　　⑱ extremely　⑲ consumption　⑳ factor
　2.　① you have experienced unwanted weight gain　（第1段落　第1文）
　　② wants to keep the brain　（第6段落　第3文）
　3.　実行可能なことで，ストレス反応やその望ましくない結果を回避する助けとなるようなことも存在する。
　　（最終段落　最終文）

ディクテーションしてみよう！の答　❶ you are not alone　❷ 50[fifty]
　❸ a steady 1.5 pounds per month　❹ anxiety and depression　❺ is an innate reaction
　❻ that will　❼ maintain a healthy lifestyle　❽ when combined with　❾ What about
　❿ be a part of life

アドバイス　❷ 15 (fifteen) と 50 (fifty) を聞き取るポイントはアクセント［強勢］の位置。fifteen は後ろ，fifty は前を強く読む。
　　thirteen / thirty や fourteen / forty なども同様。
　　❻ will などの助動詞は弱形 [wəl] と強形 [wɪl] で微妙に音が異なる。文末に置かれたり，後ろの動詞の原形が省
　　略されたりする場合は，強形の発音になる。
　　❾❿ /t/ や /d/ が母音に挟まれると「ら行」のような発音になる（⇒フラッピング）。What about は「ワラバ」，
　　part of は「パーラブ」のように聞こえる。

解 答

問1	⑤	問2	②	問3	③	問4	②
問5	⑤	問6	①	問7	⑤	問8	①
問9	③	問10	②	問11	③, ⑦		

解 説

問1

　下線部を含む部分は，need to *do*「～する必要がある」に見えるが，そうではない。the support の後に目的格の関係代名詞 which[that] が省略されており，need の後に O が欠けている。つまり，need と to *do* はつながっていない。この不定詞は副詞用法【目的】で，「～するために」の意。

①「その通りには誰一人として人が見えなかった」

▶ be to *do* は助動詞的な働きをし，【義務】【予定】【可能】【意図】【運命】の意味を表す。ここでは【可能】の意味(一般に，否定文で，to 不定詞が受け身形の場合は【可能】の意味になる)。

②「冷たい飲み物をください」

▶ to drink は形容詞用法で，「～するための」の意味。直訳すると，「飲むための冷たい何かを私にください」となる。

③「ぜひともハワイを訪れたい」

▶ would like to *do* で「～したい」の意味。この to 不定詞は like に対する目的語となっており，名詞用法。

④「実を言うと，私はニンジンが好きではない」

▶ to tell (you) the truth は「実を言うと」の意味の慣用表現(副詞用法)。このような慣用表現を独立不定詞という。

⑤**「金メダルを獲得するためには，さらなるトレーニングが不可欠だ」**

▶ 副詞用法で「～するために」という【目的】を表している。

問2

far from (being) ~ は「決して~ではない，~にはほど遠い」の意味を表す慣用表現。強い否定を表す。ここでは，universal「普遍的な，全世界(共通)の」を否定し，直後の culture-based「文化に基づく」と対比の関係にしている。

問3

(ウ)That was the hard lesson ... とあるので，第1段落から探す。③が第1段落最終文と一致し，その他の選択肢はいずれも書かれていない。

問4

下線部(エ)は仮定法の表現。I wish S had *done* ~ は「Sが~すればよかったのに」の意味で，過去の事実に反する願望を表す。この時点で，選択肢を②と③に絞れる。get under *one's* skin は「~をイライラさせる」の意味の熟語だが，この知識がなくても推測可能。第7，8段落で，ウィリアムズが役員の質問にいらだってしまい，それが原因でプレゼンテーションが失敗に終わったという内容が述べられている。よって，正解は②。

問5

下線部(オ)の that は recommendations という名詞の直後にあるので，同格の接続詞か関係代名詞と考える。後ろを見ると，she felt の後の would meet に対するSがない。そこで，関係代名詞とわかる。なお，she felt が関係代名詞の直後に挿入されているが，このようなパターンを連鎖関係詞節という（→ p.154 参照）。

① 「彼女はフランス語のネイティブスピーカーであるようだ」

▶ that は接続詞。It は【状況】を表す用法で，It が S，seems が V，that 以下が C。It は形式主語ではない。It seems that ... で「…ようだ」の意味。

② 「あなたが**無事にここに**到着したことを彼女はとても喜んでいる」

▶ that は接続詞。感情の後に続く that 節は【感情の原因】を表す副詞節。

③ 「お金をすべて古着に費やすとは，彼はおかしいに違いない」

▶ that は接続詞で，that 節は【判断の根拠】を表す副詞節。「…するとは」の意。

④「試験に合格するためにもっと一生懸命勉強しなさい」

▶ that は接続詞で, so that … は「…するために」という【目的】を表す副詞節。that 節内では助動詞 can / may / will が用いられる。

⑤「バラの育て方を教えてくれる本を貸してください」

▶ 名詞の直後にあり, will tell に対する S が欠けるので that は関係代名詞。

問6

〈疑問詞＋to do〉で「(疑問詞の訳)〜すべきか」の意味を表す。各選択肢の意味は, how to do「どのように〜すべきか → 〜する方法」, when to do「いつ〜すべきか」, which to do「どちらを〜すべきか」, where to do「どこで〜すべきか」となる(why to do という形はない)。

文の後半にある分詞構文(practicing her arguments, anticipating questions that might arise, and preparing responses to those questions「自分の主張を練習し, 生じる質問を予測し, それらの質問に対する応答を準備した」)の内容および本文の主題が「説得術」「説得の手法」であることから how to が適切。

問7

非制限用法〈, (コンマ) ＋関係詞〉の which は, 前の節全体または一部を指す。下線部の後に puzzled and annoyed me「私を困惑させ, イライラさせた」と続くので, which はネガティブな内容を指す。よって, which が指す内容は I got the feeling that they were attacking my research ability「彼らが私の調査能力を攻撃しているような気持ちになった」と考えられ, ⑤が正解となる。

問8

下線部(ク)の前までの内容を見ると, 第7段落後半で, ウィリアムズは, 高度な知識を持つ専門家である自分に対して, プレゼンテーションの聞き手である会社役員たちが敬意の欠けた態度を取っていることに不満を述べている。下線部(ク)は What rudeness to think that … となっているが, 省略を補うと, What rudeness it is to think that … となり, What は感嘆詞, it が形式主語で to think 以下が真主語。rudeness は rude「失礼な」の名詞形。「…と考えるのはなんと失礼なことか」の意味。以上により, 正解は①。

問9

　下線部の意味は「今では彼らの手法によって私が要点からそれてしまうのを許してしまったことを後悔している」。kick *oneself* for 〜 は「〜のことで自分を責める，悔やむ」の意味。run *A* off *B* は「A を B からそらす，退かせる」。これらの熟語を知らなかったとしても，第8段落はプレゼンテーションの失敗へのウィリアムズの感想を述べていること，ウィリアムズの経験についての記述が始まる第2段落で失敗に対する後悔の念が示されていることから，選択肢は①と③に絞れる。①は「彼らのやり方を利用して」の部分が文意に合わない。

問10

　go down the drain で「水の泡になる，無駄になる」。これを知らなくても，プレゼンテーションは失敗に終わり，提案は承認されなかったのだから，準備が無駄になったことがわかる。正解は②「無駄に費やされた」。他の選択肢の意味は，①「報われた」，③「成果があった」，④「かなり役立った」，⑤「削減された」。

問11

①▶ 第1段落第1文と合致しない。

②▶ 第2段落第1文と合致しない。正しくは，アメリカからドイツに来た。

③▶ 第3段落第2文と合致するので正解。

④▶ 第5段落第2文と合致しない。いきなり本題に入ったとあるので，前置きはしなかったことになる。

⑤▶ 第5段落第3文と合致しない。終わる前に質問をし始めている。

⑥▶ 第8段落第1文と合致しない。防御的になった結果，プレゼンテーションが失敗に終わったとある。

⑦▶ 第9段落と合致するので正解。

第1段落　文の構造と語句のチェック

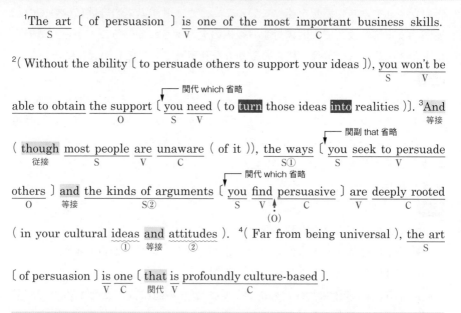

¹The art〔of persuasion〕is one of the most important business skills.
S ── V ── C

²(Without the ability〔to persuade others to support your ideas〕), you won't be
S ── V

── 関代 which 省略

able to obtain the support〔you need（to turn those ideas into realities）〕. ³And
O ── S ── V ── 等接

── 関副 that 省略

(though most people are unaware (of it)), the ways〔you seek to persuade
従接 ── S ── V ── C ── S① ── S ── V

── 関代 which 省略

others〕and the kinds of arguments〔you find persuasive〕are deeply rooted
O ── 等接 ── S② ── S ── V ── C ── V ── C
　　　　　　　　　　　　　　　　　　　　　　(O)

(in your cultural ideas and attitudes). ⁴(Far from being universal), the art
① 等接 ② ── S

〔of persuasion〕is one〔that is profoundly culture-based〕.
V ── C ── 関代 ── V ── C

> 訳 ¹説得術は，最も重要なビジネススキルの1つだ。²他の人々に自分の考えを支持しても
> らうよう説得する能力がなければ，それらの考えを現実にするためにあなたが必要とする
> 支持を得ることができないだろう。³そして，多くの人々が気づいていないことであるが，
> 他の人を説得しようとする方法や，説得力があるとあなたが思うような主張は，文化的な
> 考え方や態度に深く根差している。⁴説得術は決して普遍的なものではなく，深く文化に基
> づいている。

語句

art	名 技術	
persuasion	名 説得	
ability	名 能力	

persuade	動 説得する	
support	動 支持する／名 支持	
obtain	動 得る，獲得する	
turn _A_ into _B_	熟 AをBに変える	

146

reality	名	現実
be unaware of ~	熟	~に気づいていない
seek to *do*	熟	~しようとする
argument	名	主張，論拠
persuasive	形	説得力のある
be rooted in ~	熟	~に根差している

cultural	形	文化的な
attitude	名	態度，姿勢
far from (being) ~		
	熟	決して~ではない，~にはほど遠い
universal	形	普遍的な，全世界(共通)の
profoundly	副	深く，大いに

第2段落　文の構造と語句のチェック

¹That was the hard lesson 〔 learned by Kara Williams, an American engineer
S　V　　　C　　　　　　　　　　　　　　└────同格────┘

〔 newly employed (as a research manager for a German automobile firm)〕〕.

²(As one of the leading experts in her field), Williams had extensive experience
　　　　　　　　　　　　　　　　　　　　　　　S　　V　　　O

┌── 前置詞 in 省略　　　　　　　　┌── 前置詞 in 省略
〔 presenting recommendations 〕 and 〔 influencing her American colleagues to
①　　　　　　　　　　　　　　等接 ②

follow her ideas 〕.　³But (when Williams began working (in a German
　　　　　　　　　　等接　従接　S　　V　　O

environment)), she didn't realize 〈 that 〈 being persuasive 〉 would require a
　　　　　　　　　　S　　V　　O 従接 S　　　　　　　　　V

different approach 〉.　⁴"(When I think back (to my first presentation 〔 to my
　　O　　　　　　　　　　従接 S　　V

new German bosses])), I wish 〈 I had understood the difference and hadn't let
　　　　　　　　　　　S V O S　　V①　　　　O　　等接　V②

their feedback get under my skin 〉.　⁵(If I had been cool enough) I might have
　　O　　　C　　　　　　　　　　従接 S　V　　C　　　S　　V

been able to save the situation."
　　　　　O

訳 ¹それは，新しくドイツの自動車会社の研究マネージャーとして雇われたアメリカ人の
エンジニア，カラ・ウィリアムズが学んだ厳しい教訓だった。² 自分の分野での第一線の
専門家の１人として，ウィリアムズは提案を発表したり，自分の考えに従うようにアメリ
カ人の同僚に影響を与えることを幅広く経験した。³しかし，ウィリアムズがドイツの環境
で働き始めたとき，説得力を持つためには異なるアプローチが必要だということに気づか
なかった。⁴「新しいドイツ人の上司への最初のプレゼンテーションを思い返すと，その違
いを理解し，彼らの反応にいらだたなければよかったのにと思います。⁵もし十分な冷静さ
を持っていれば，事態を収拾できたかもしれませんでした」

語句

lesson	名	教訓
engineer	名	エンジニア，技術者
employ	動	雇う，用いる，使用する
research	名	研究，調査
German	形	ドイツ(人)の
automobile	名	自動車
firm	名	会社
leading	形	一流の，第一線の
expert	名	専門家
field	名	分野
extensive	形	広範囲にわたる
present	動	発表する，プレゼンテーションする
recommendation	名	提案，助言

influence	動	影響を与える
colleague	名	同僚
follow	動	従う
environment	名	周囲の状況，環境
realize	動	わかる，気づく
require	動	必要とする
approach	名	取り組み方，手法
think back to ～	熟	～を思い返す，振り返る
presentation	名	発表，プレゼンテーション
feedback	名	反応，反響
get under *one's* skin	熟	～を悩ませる，イライラさせる
cool	形	冷静な
save	動	救う
situation	名	状況，事態

第３段落　文の構造と語句のチェック

¹Williams' first project was 〈 providing technical advice 〔 on 〈 how to reduce
　　　S　　　　　　　　V　　C　　V′　　　O′

carbon emissions from one of the group's "green" car models 〉〕〉.　²〈 After

〈 visiting several automobile plants 〉, 〈 observing the systems and processes
①　　　　　　　　　　　　　　　　　　②　　　　　　　　　　①　　等接　②

there 〉, and 〈 meeting with dozens of experts and users 〉〉, Williams developed a
　　　等接 ③　　　　　　　　　　　　　　①　　等接　②　　　　　S　　　　V

set of recommendations 〔 that she felt would meet the company's goals 〕. ³She
　　　　　O　　　　　　　　関代 S　V　　V　　　　　　　O　　　　　　　　　S

〔挿入〕

traveled (to Munich) (to give a one-hour presentation (to the decision makers
　V

— a group of German directors)).

〔同格〕

> **訳** ¹ウィリアムズの最初のプロジェクトは，グループの「環境に優しい」車のモデルのうちの1つから，炭素排出量を削減する方法に関して技術的な助言を提供するというものだった。²彼女はいくつかの自動車工場を訪れ，そこでのシステムや工程を観察し，何十人もの専門家やユーザーと会合した後，会社の目標を達成するであろうと彼女が思う一連の提案書を作成した。³彼女は，意思決定者であるドイツ人の役員たちに1時間のプレゼンテーションを行うため，ミュンヘンに赴いた。

語句

provide	動 提供する	process	名 製法，工程
technical	形 技術的な	dozens of ~	熟 何十もの~
carbon	名 炭素	develop	動 開発する，作成する
emission	名 排出（量）	a set of ~	熟 一連の~
green	形 環境に優しい	meet	動 達成する，満たす
plant	名 （製造）工場	goal	名 目標
observe	動 観察する	decision maker	名 意思決定者
		director	名 会社役員，取締役

第4段落　文の構造と語句のチェック

¹"It was my first presentation, and its success would be important (for my
　S　V　　　C　　　　　　　等接　S　　　　　V　　　　C

reputation)," Williams recalls. ²(In preparation for the meeting), Williams
　　　　　　　　　　S　　　V　　　　　　　　　　　　　　　　　　　　　　　S

thought carefully (about 〈 how to give the most persuasive presentation 〉),
　V

(practicing her arguments), (anticipating questions 〔 that might arise 〕), and
①　　　　　　　　　　　　②　　　　　　　　　　　　　　　関代　　V　　　　　等接

(preparing responses 〔 to those questions 〕).
③

訳 ¹「それは私の最初のプレゼンテーションであり，その成功は私の評判にとって重要でした」とウィリアムズは振り返る。²会合に備え，ウィリアムズは最も説得力のあるプレゼンテーションを行う方法について注意深く考え，自分の主張を練習し，生じうる質問を予測し，それらの質問に対する応答を準備した。

語句

reputation 名 評判
recall 動 思い出す，思い出を語る
in preparation for ～
　　　　　熟 ～に備えて，～に向けて準備して

anticipate
　　　　　動 予期する，予測して対策を講ずる
arise 動 生じる
response 名 回答，応答

第5段落 文の構造と語句のチェック

¹Williams delivered her presentation (in a small hall 〔 with the directors
　S　　　　V　　　　O　　　　　　　　　　　　　　　　　　　　　　　S′

seated (in rows of chairs)〕). ²She began (by getting right to the
V′　　　　　　　　　　　　　　　　　　　　S　　V

　　　　　　　　　　　　　　　　　　　── 関代 which 省略
point), (explaining the strategies 〔 she would recommend (based on her
　　　　　　　　　　　　　　　　　　　　　S　　　V

findings)〕). ³But (before she had finished (with the first part)), one of the
　　　　　　　　　等接　従接　S　　V　　　　　　　　　　　　　　　　　S
　　　　　　　　　But
directors raised his hand and protested, "How did you get (to these
　　　　　V①　　O　　等接　V②　　　　　　　(V)　S　V

conclusions)? ⁴You are giving us your recommendations, but I don't understand
　　　　　　　　S　　V　　O₁　　O₂　　　　　　等接　S　　V

〈 how you got here 〉. ⁵How many people did you interview? ⁶What questions
O　疑　S　V　　　　　　　　　　O　　　　　(V)　S　V　　　　　　O

did you ask?"
(V)　S　V

150

訳 ¹ウィリアムズは並んだ椅子に役員たちが座っている小さなホールでプレゼンテーションを行った。²彼女は初めにいきなり本題に入り，自分の調査結果に基づいて推奨する戦略を説明した。³しかし，最初の部分が終わる前に，役員の一人が手を上げて抗議した。「どのようにしてこれらの結論に至ったのですか？ ⁴あなたは私たちに提案をしていますが，あなたがどのようにそこに至ったのか理解できません。⁵あなたは何人の人と面談しましたか？ ⁶どのような質問をしましたか？」

語句

deliver
　　動（演説，プレゼンテーションなどを）行う
hall　　名 広間，ホール
seat　　動 座らせる
row　　名 列，並び
get to the point 熟 本題に入る，ズバリ言う
　　（*get right[straight] to the point で「ただちに本題に入る，単刀直入に言う」の意味）

explain　　動 説明する
strategy　　名 戦略
recommend 動 推奨する
based on ~　熟 ～に基づいて
finding　　名 調査結果，所見
finish with ~ 熟 ～を済ませる，終わらせる
protest　　動 抗議する
conclusion　名 結論
interview　　動 面談する，面接する

第6段落　文の構造と語句のチェック

¹Then another director jumped in: ²"Please explain 〈 what methods you used （ for analyzing your data 〉〉 and 〈 how that led you to come to these findings 〉."

訳 ¹その後，別の役員が割り込んで言った。²「あなたがデータを分析するためにどんな方法を使用したか，それがどのようにしてあなたをこれらの調査結果に至らせたのかを説明してください」

語句
jump in　　熟（会話に）割り込む
method　　名 方法

analyze　　動 分析する
data　　名 データ

¹"I was shocked," Williams remembers. ²"I assured them 〈 that the methods
　S　V　　C　　　　S　　　　V　　　　　S　　V　　O₁　O₂〈従接〉　　　　　S

〔behind my recommendations〕 were sound 〉, but the questions and challenges
　　　　　　　　　　　　　　　　V　　C　等接　①　　　S　　等接②

continued. ³The more they questioned me, the more I got the feeling 〈 that they
　V　　　　　　　　　S　　V　　O　　　　　　　S　V　　O　　　　　〈従接 S
　　　　　　　　　　　　　　　　　　　　　　　　　　　　　　　　　（同格）

were attacking my research ability 〉, which puzzled and annoyed me. ⁴I am an
　V　　　　　　O　　　　　　　　　　関代　①　　等接②　　　　O　　S　V
　　

experienced specialist 〔in engineering〕〔with a lot of know-how 〔that is widely
　　　　　　C　　　　　　　　　　　　　　　　　　　　　　　　　　関代

acknowledged 〕〕. ⁵Their effort 〔to test my conclusions〕,（I felt）, showed a real
　V　　　　　　　　　S　　　　　　　　　　　　　　　S　V　　　V　　O

lack of respect. ⁶What rudeness 〈 to think 〈 that they would be better able to
　　　　　　感　　　C　　真S　V　　従接　S　　　　V

judge than I am 〉〉!"

訳 ¹「私はショックを受けました」とウィリアムズは回想する。²「私の提案の裏付けとなる方法が適切であることを彼らに保証しましたが、質問や異議は続きました。³彼らが私に質問をするほど、彼らが私の調査能力を攻撃しているような気持ちになり、そのことが私を困惑させ、イライラさせました。⁴私は、広く認められた専門知識を多く持っている、経験豊富な工学の専門家です。⁵彼らが私の結論を検証しようと試みるなんて、まさしく敬意の欠如を示していると私は感じました。⁶彼らが私よりも優れた判断ができると思うなんて、なんと失礼なことでしょう！」

語句

assure	動	保証する、納得させる	specialist	名 専門家
sound	形	適切な、信頼できる	engineering	名 エンジニアリング、工学
challenge	名	異議、説明要求	know-how	名 専門知識、ノウハウ
puzzle	動	困らせる、悩ませる	effort	名 努力、試み
annoy	動	イライラさせる	lack	名 欠如
experienced	形	経験豊富な	respect	名 尊重、敬意
			rudeness	名 失礼、無礼

第8段落 文の構造と語句のチェック

¹Williams reacted defensively, and the presentation began collapsing (from
 S   V   等接   S   V   O

there). ²"I kick myself now (for having allowed their approach to run me off
        S V O   V'   O'   C'

my point)," she says. ³(Needless to say), they did not approve my
         S   V   S V

recommendations, and three months of research time went (down the drain)."
 O   等接   S   V

訳 ¹ウィリアムズは防御的な反応を示し，プレゼンテーションはそこから崩れ始めた。²「今
では彼らの手法によって私が要点からそれてしまうのを許してしまったことを後悔してい
ます」と彼女は言う。³「言うまでもなく，彼らは私の提案を承認せず，３カ月間の調査時
間が水の泡になりました」

語句

react 　　　動 反応する
defensively 　副 防御的に
collapse 　　動 崩れる，崩壊する
kick *oneself* for ~
　　　　　　熟 ~のことで自分を責める，悔やむ

run *A* off *B* 　熟 A を B からそらす，退かせる
needless to say 熟 言うまでもなく
approve 　　動 承認する
go down the drain
　　　　　　熟 水の泡になる，無駄になる

第9段落 文の構造と語句のチェック

　　　　　┌─ 関代 which 省略
¹The stone wall [Williams ran into] illustrates the hard truth 〈 that our
 S   S   V   V   O   従接(同格) S

ability [to persuade others] depends not only (on the strength of our message)
                     V

but (on 〈 how we build our arguments 〉 and the persuasive techniques [we
①   関副 S V   O   等接   ②   S

employ])).
 V

語句

stone wall 名 石壁(越えがたい障害の比喩)	**depend on ~**
run into ~ 熟 ~にぶち当たる，~に出くわす	熟 ~によって決まる，~に左右される
illustrate 動 例証する，例示する	**strength** 名 強さ
	build 動 組み立てる，構築する

文法事項の整理 ⑫ 連鎖関係詞節

第3段落第2文の that についてみてみよう。

..., Williams developed a set of recommendations **that** she felt would meet the company's goals.

関係詞の直後に，〈S＋V(＝that 節をとれる動詞)〉が挿入されることがある。これを「連鎖関係詞節」という。

例 He is a boy who *I believe* is honest.
「彼は，正直者だと私が信じている少年だ」

＊ここで，who の部分を whom とするのは誤り。この英文は，He is a boy.＋I believe (that) *he* is honest. という2つの英文が合体したものだから，主格の代名詞 he に対応する主格の関係代名詞 who にしなければならない。

＊この who は主格であるが省略できる。

＊この英文は以下のように書き換え可。

He is a boy whom I believe honest.

(← He is a boy. ＋ I believe *him* honest.)

例 You should do what *you think* is right.
　「あなたは自分が正しいと思うことをすべきだ」
＊この what は主格。
＊この英文は以下のように書き換え可。こちらの what は目的格（think
　は第5文型）。
　You should do what you think right.

例 John, who *I remembered* was good at math, is majoring in physics
　now.
　「ジョンは，私の記憶では数学が得意だったが，今は物理学を専攻し
　ている」
＊非制限用法の例。

例 I will do everything (that) *I expect* you can't do.
　「君ができないと予想されることは何でもやってあげるつもりだ」
＊目的格の例。

例 There are many cases where *I think* this rule does not apply.
　「このルールがあてはまらないと思われる場合が数多く存在する」
＊関係副詞の例。

■第3段落第2文
..., Williams developed a set of recommendations <u>that</u> she felt would
meet the company's goals.
▶関係代名詞 that の後に she felt という〈S＋V〉が挿入されている（連鎖
　関係詞節）。その後には would meet という V が続くので，この関係代
　名詞 that は主格だとわかる。

確認問題

1. 次の和訳と対応する英語の語句を，頭文字を参考にして書き，空欄を完成させよう。

（各1点×20）

① o ⬜　　　　**動** 得る，獲得する

② be r ⬜ in 〜　　**熟** 〜に根差している

③ u ⬜　　　　**形** 普遍的な，全世界(共通)の

④ e ⬜　　　　**動** 雇う，用いる，使用する

⑤ l ⬜　　　　**形** 一流の，第一線の

⑥ e ⬜　　　　**形** 広範囲にわたる

⑦ c ⬜　　　　**名** 同僚

⑧ e ⬜　　　　**名** 排出(量)

⑨ o ⬜　　　　**動** 観察する

⑩ r ⬜　　　　**名** 評判

⑪ a ⬜　　　　**動** 予期する，

　　　　　　　　　　予測して対策を講ずる

⑫ b ⬜ on 〜　　**熟** 〜に基づいて

⑬ p ⬜　　　　**動** 抗議する

⑭ c ⬜　　　　**名** 結論

⑮ a ⬜　　　　**動** 分析する

⑯ e ⬜　　　　**形** 経験豊富な

⑰ c ⬜　　　　**動** 崩れる，崩壊する

⑱ n ⬜ to s ⬜　**熟** 言うまでもなく

⑲ i ⬜　　　　**動** 例証する，例示する

⑳ s ⬜　　　　**名** 強さ

2. 次の[　]内の語句を並べ替えて，意味の通る英文を完成させよう。（各5点×2）

① She [right / to / by / the / getting / began / point], explaining the strategies she would recommend based on her findings.

② [questioned / more / the / they / me], the more I got the feeling that they were attacking my research ability, which puzzled and annoyed me.

3. 次の英文を和訳してみよう。(10 点)

Williams developed a set of recommendations that she felt would meet the company's goals.

＊Williams「ウィリアムズ」

ディクテーションしてみよう！

今回学習した英文に出てきた語句・表現を，＿＿＿に書き取ろう。

65,73

65 The art of persuasion is one of the most important business skills. Without the ability to persuade others to support your ideas, you won't be able to obtain the support you need to turn those ideas into realities. And though ❶＿＿＿＿＿＿＿＿＿＿＿＿＿＿＿＿＿＿＿＿＿, the ways you seek to persuade others and the kinds of arguments you find persuasive are deeply rooted in your cultural ideas and attitudes. Far from being universal, the art of persuasion is one that is profoundly culture-based.

66 That was the hard lesson learned by Kara Williams, an American engineer newly employed as a research manager for a German automobile firm. As one of the leading experts in her field, Williams had extensive experience presenting recommendations and influencing her American colleagues to follow her ideas. But when Williams began working in a German environment, she didn't realize that being persuasive would require a different approach. "When I think back to my first presentation to my new German bosses, I wish I had understood the difference and hadn't let their feedback get under my skin. If I had been cool enough I ❷＿＿＿＿＿＿＿＿＿＿＿＿＿＿＿＿＿＿ save the situation."

67   Williams' first project was providing technical advice on how to reduce carbon emissions from one of the group's "green" car models. After visiting several automobile plants, observing the systems and processes there, and meeting with dozens of experts and users, Williams developed a set of recommendations ❸_____ the company's goals.   She traveled to Munich to give a one-hour presentation to the decision makers — a group of German directors.

68   "It was my first presentation, and its success would be important for my reputation," Williams recalls.   In preparation for the meeting, Williams thought carefully about how to give the most persuasive presentation, practicing   her   arguments,   ❹_____

_____, and preparing responses to those questions.

69   Williams delivered her presentation in a small hall with the directors seated in rows of chairs.   She began by getting right to the point, explaining the strategies she would recommend ❺_____

_____.   But before she had finished with the first part, one of the directors raised his hand and protested, "How did you get to these conclusions? You are giving us your recommendations, but I don't understand how you got here.   How many people did you interview?   What questions did you ask?"

70   Then another director ❻_____: "Please explain what methods you used for analyzing your data and how that led you to come to these findings."

71   "I was shocked," Williams remembers.   "I assured them that the methods behind my recommendations were sound, but the questions and challenges continued.   The more they questioned me, the more I got the feeling that they were attacking my research ability, which puzzled and annoyed me.   I am an experienced specialist in engineering with a lot of know-how that is widely acknowledged.   Their effort to test my conclusions, I felt, showed ❼_____.   What rudeness to think that they would be better able to judge than I am!"

72　Williams reacted defensively, and the presentation began collapsing from there. "I kick myself now for having allowed their approach to run me off my point," she says. "**❽**_____, they did not approve my recommendations, and three months of research time went down the drain."

73　The stone wall Williams ran into **❾**_____ _____ that our ability to persuade others depends not only on the strength of our message but on how we build our arguments and the persuasive techniques we employ.

確認問題の答　**1.** ① obtain　② rooted　③ universal　④ employ　⑤ leading
⑥ extensive　⑦ colleague　⑧ emission　⑨ observe　⑩ reputation
⑪ anticipate　⑫ based　⑬ protest　⑭ conclusion　⑮ analyze　⑯ experienced
⑰ collapse　⑱ needless, say　⑲ illustrate　⑳ strength
2. ① began by getting right to the point　(第5段落　第2文)
② The more they questioned me　(第7段落　第3文)
3. ウィリアムズは会社の目標を達成するであろうと彼女が思う一連の提案書を作成した。(第3段落　第2文)

ディクテーションしてみよう！の答　❶ most people are unaware of it　❷ might have been able to
❸ that she felt would meet　❹ anticipating questions that might arise
❺ based on her findings　❻ jumped in　❼ a real lack of respect　❽ Needless to say
❾ illustrates the hard truth
アドバイス　❷ been の n の音と，able の a がつながり，「ネイ」のように聞こえる (⇒連結)。
❸連鎖関係詞節のパターン (関係詞＋S′ ＋V′ ＋V ～) を理解しておけば聞き取りやすくなる。
❾2つの子音 (hard の d，truth の t) が隣り合うことにより，前の子音 (d) がほぼ聞こえなくなる (⇒脱落)。